Writing Like a Journali

MW00929603

Notes, Notations and Notions on the Craft of Writing

James Glen Stovall

Tennessee Journalism Series

First Inning Press

in conjunction with the

Intercollegiate Online News Network

Table of Contents

Forward

Good writing is at the heart of journalism.

Journalists write for a living. They use words precisely and efficiently. They present accurate, verified information in a way that a mass audience will understand it by reading or hearing it only once.

Such writing takes skill, discipline and practice.

Writing Like a Journalist will give you some of the basic concepts of how journalists achieve good writing -- writing that an audience can understand and will pay for.

Author

James Glen Stovall has taught journalism at UT since 2006. Previously he taught at the University of Alabama and Emory and Henry College. He is the author of numerous books, including *Writing for the Mass Media*. More information: http://jem.cci.utk.edu/users/james-glen-stovall

The designer of the iPad edition of this book is **Chelsea Jensen Koerten**. She is a multimedia student journalist at the University of Tennessee. A Chancellor Scholar, she is assisting the author of this book and others of the Tennessee Journalism Series as part of her honors thesis project.

Tennessee Journalism Series

This book is a part of the **Tennessee Journalism Series**.

The Tennessee Journalism Series is a set of texts and instructional material developed by the faculty of the University of Tennessee School of Journalism and Electronic Media for journalism instructors around the world.

The idea behind the series is "multimedia first."

That is, these books are built for the iPad and contain a variety of multimedia elements: text, audio, video, photo galleries, interactive images, and interactive reviews and quizzes.

At present, eight books are available on the iBookstore for downloading to an iPad:

- **Introduction to Journalism**

- **Reporting: An Introduction**

- **Photojournalism**

- **The First Amendment**

- **Feature Writing**

- **Media Reporting**

- **Going Online**

- **Writing Like a Journalist**

Other books under development include texts on sports journalism, how to get a job on television, social media and journalism, audio journalism and video journalism. Various aspects of the history of journalism will also be part of this series.

(March 2013)

The Discipline of Good Writing

Writing is something that everyone does but few people do well. Those who do it well have either "natural talent" or the discipline to learn the principles and apply them to everything they write.

It started with the Sumerians

The earliest writing that is anything close to what we do today comes from the Sumerians, the ancient civilization that occupied the Tigris and Euphrates valley (now Iraq and Iran) more than 3,000 years ago. Paper and ink as we know it were nonexistent in that part of the world. Instead, the Sumerians made soft clay tablets and used some kind of pointed instrument to impress upon these tablets a set of symbols they had developed to represent the information ideas they wanted to record. These tablets hardened into permanent records, and we in the twenty-first century have been the lucky inheritors of a few of them – enough to know a little about what the Sumerians were like.

Archeologists have figured out enough about Sumerian writing to translate the first story we have in writing, The Epic of Gilgamesh. The story – the journeys of a legendary hero of the time – has drawn the widest attention to the writing of the Sumerians and is even considered to be in the realm of literature.

But much of the writing of Sumerians has nothing to do with literature. Most of the tablets we possess are simply recordings of the everyday concerns of the Sumerians. They contain information about what was grown and stored, how buildings should be constructed and a variety of other mundane concerns.

These early writers went to great pains to record this information. Preparing and writing on a clay tablet was undoubtedly much more difficult than firing up a computer or grabbing a pen and a sheet of paper. Yet these ancients wrote with care and precision. They tried to get it right. They tried to get down good information that they could refer to and that others could use.

They did this not because they thought that distant civilizations such as ours would be reading their work 3,000 years after it was produced. Rather, they went to the trouble to write things down because it was important to them at the time, and it was important that they pass on information to their contemporaries and immediate successors. These ancient authors certainly believed that what they were doing was beneficial to them and to their society. They approached the job of writing with a serious purpose in mind.

So should we.

The importance of writing

Writing is one of the most important inventions – if not the most important invention – of human beings. Without it, our culture and our personal lives would be seriously restricted to the ideas and information that we could receive orally and remember. Writing helps us preserve what we know and think and gives it an exactitude that could not be achieved otherwise. Writing forms the basis of our lives and our activities, both cosmic and daily.

Yet, most of us take writing for granted.

We know that it is important because it is a skill that we learn early in our formal education. We use that skill continuously through our educational, professional and personal lives. We learn various forms of writing – from text messaging to formal term papers for our courses – that are appropriate for the situations in which we write. But few of us take the time to examine the process by which we write or to try to improve our writing skills. As long as we can get our thoughts and ideas across to the person reading our writing, we feel satisfied that we have accomplished what is necessary.

In this "age of communication," however, simply making contact with our readers is not enough. The rudiments of writing that we learned, more or less, as young children are not adequate to the demands that we face as adults. We have to learn to do better, to express our information and ideas with more precision and efficiency than we did in the second grade.

That's why this book exists.

Journalists, first and foremost, are writers. Good journalism means gathering important, interesting and timely information and writing it in a way that people will read, understand and even enjoy. Journalists must accomplish this task quickly, sometimes within a few minutes.

People who can do this are relatively rare, and journalists and those in related professions are highly valued because they have knowledge about how to use the language effectively. In other words, you can make your living by writing like a journalist.

ESSAY: My friend Fowler

Early in my academic writing career, I met Fowler.

I was putting together the first edition of *Writing for the Mass Media* and was looking for some basic writing references and somehow -- I don't remember how -- came upon Fowler. It was, in the parlance of that day, the real thing. Fowler is an "it," as well as a "he."

He is Henry Fowler. It is *A Dictionary of Modern English Usage*, or as Jim Holt noted in his essay in the New York Times, (http://www.nytimes.com/2009/12/13/books/review/Holt-t.html?ref=books&_r=1&) "among its devotees it is known, reverentially, as 'Fowler.'"

Holt told the interesting story of how Fowler the "he" became Fowler the "it." Henry Fowler was a former school teacher and amateur wordsmith who lived on the island of Guernsey with his younger brother Frank. In the first decade of the 20th century, Henry and Frank published a book titled *The King's English*, which, despite their amateur status, was a great success. They took on the editing of *The Concise Oxford Dictionary* and then planned a larger book on the language, but World War I occurred. Frank died of tuberculosis, and Henry barely survived a bout of illness. But when he did, he took up the project that he and his brother had envisioned.

As Holt related in his essay:

The book was published in 1926, to immediate acclaim and brisk sales. Although language, as the truism goes, is an ever changing Heraclitean river, Fowler was not revised until 1965, when Sir Ernest Gowers gave it a light going-over, preserving both the spirit and the substance of the original. (The same cannot be said of the 1996 third edition, heavily reworked by R. W. Burchfield.) Now Oxford University Press has reissued the classic first edition of A Dictionary of Modern English Usage ($29.95), with an acute new introduction by the linguist David Crystal. **It is a volume that everyone who aspires to a better command of English should possess and consult —** *sparingly.* (emphasis mine)

Sparingly, as Holt pointed out in the rest of his essay, is the key.

You can't take Fowler too seriously because, for one, Fowler doesn't take himself too seriously. The language should be whatever is useful and not laden with a lot of half-wit rules (such as never splitting an infinitive).

The dictionary isn't a dictionary of definitions but rather a collection of short essays on the language. Most of them are short, thought-provoking, delightful and informative.

Writing for an audience

Journalists write for an audience, not themselves.

The audience – its expectations and inclinations – should be foremost in the mind of the writer whenever he or she begins the process of composition.

We also owe it to ourselves to write well. A continuing theme of this book is that what we write reveals a great deal about us both personally and professionally. The messages that we send with our writing go far beyond the content of the composition. They tell our audience how much we know, how we think and how highly we regard them. Take, again, the note home to parents. If it is written carelessly and contains errors or if it leaves out information that should be included, that may signal to the reader that we lack the skill to compose a note properly. Or that we simply do not care very much about the reader.

I once received the following email from a student who wanted to know how she had done on a quiz. The quiz had been given on a computer, and she was supposed to email her answers to the professor:

> *Ihavent recieved my test grade from our first exam , we usually would have gotten them by now , I was just wanting to make sure that there wasnt a problem with my email , maybe I typed it in wrong, let me know.*

What does this note saying about the student – especially considering that the course she was in was devoted to improving writing? When this student was made aware of how badly the email was written, she excused herself by saying it was only "internet typing," whatever that means.

Figuring out what the student wanted was not the problem. Despite her lousy composition, it was easy to understand that she wanted to know about her grade.

But her note reveals volumes about her attitude and understanding of the importance of good writing skills. That she would write a note to her writing teacher in such a slovenly way fairly shouted, "I DON'T HAVE ANY SKILLS, AND I DON'T UNDERSTAND WHAT THIS IS ALL ABOUT!"

And it would not be unreasonable to read another message into this: "I don't really care very much."

ESSAY: Invisible writing

Before his untimely death in 2009, one of the best mystery novelists around was William G. Tapply, creator of the Brady Coyne mystery series.

Tapply's novels live up to the cover blurbs -- well-formed characters, tightly woven plots and elegant writing.

Tapply practiced what many of us who teach writing often preach, and he gives voice to some of those practices in an essay on his web site called "Invisible Writing."

The essay tells the story of what Tapply learned from his father -- also an excellent writer -- when he was beginning his craft. The essay emphasizes two major points I make with my students:

-- pay attention to verbs (read more on this) and

-- try to make your writing invisible to the reader.

The term I use for the second point is "modesty." A good writer should try to put the content in the foreground and the writer in the background.

Tapply's essay and his novels are well worth reading.

Characteristics of good writing

All good writing in a professional realm shares four characteristics: accuracy, clarity, precision and efficiency. A good writer should have a clear sense of the necessity of achieving these characteristics in every piece of writing he or she undertakes. Writers can develop good habits that will make it easer to compose communications that are clear and understandable, that do not waste the time and effort of readers, and that give readers the information they need and expect.

Accuracy

Anyone who writes something with the expectation that someone else will read it enters into a relationship with that person. It is a relationship of trust. The writer is saying, "Let me have your time and attention. If you give me that, I will tell you something that is interesting or important to you. Based on my position or knowledge, I have the authority to ask this of you. What I have to say to you will be true in the sense that both you and I understand it."

Early in 2006 best-selling author James Frey was found to have violated that trust. He had written a book titled *A Million Little Pieces*, an account of his descent into drug addiction. His compelling prose – and an endorsement from talk show maven Oprah Winfrey – boosted to the book to one of the top selling titles of 2005. Frey had told his story with compelling prose, but the most compelling thing about his story was not the prose. It was the fact that it was true. At least, he said it was true.

The Smoking Gun website investigated Frey's claims about being jailed for several months and found that he had spent only a few hours in a lockup. Other claims that Frey had made also turned out to be false. Frey admitted that parts of his book were the products of his imagination, not a true story as he had insisted in many interviews promoting the book. For a time, Frey was defended by Winfrey and others who should have known better. Eventually, however, many of Frey's defenders came to see that he had broken a trust with his readers.

Accuracy, then, means more than just getting facts and information right. It means living up to the trust that readers place in you.

Clarity

Clarity is also a hallmark of good writing. In the professional world, readers should not have to "figure out" what a writer means. Readers should not have to read something twice in order to understand it.

Clarity stems from writing as simply as possible – using words and phrases that readers are certain to understand. Writers should treat readers as intelligent beings whose time is valuable. Their prose should be as straightforward as possible. Benjamin Franklin, one of the great writers of his day, once advised, "To write clearly, not only the most expressive, but the plainest words should be chosen."

One of the keys to clarity in writing is for the writer to withdraw as much as possible from the writing itself. That is, as a professional, the writer should not be tempted to inject his or her personality into the writing itself. A writer should be modest, making sure that readers see the information and purpose of the writing rather than the writer.

Achieving clarity, simplicity and modesty in writing is not an easy thing to do. The novelist W. Somerset Maugham captured the difficulty perfectly when he said, "To write simply is as difficult as to be good." Simple, elegant prose is easy to spot and easy to read. It also appears easy to produce. Nothing could be further from the truth. Whenever we write, our minds are cluttered with many different thoughts, ideas and pieces of information. Our brains race along much faster than our hands can move a pen or even our fingers can type. All of us have to work hard at being simple, straightforward and clear. Yet there are ways we can improve our clarity in writing by developing an understanding of what clarity means and forming good writing – and good thinking – habits.

ESSAY: Simple words

Should a journalist try to build a large vocabulary?

One of the things good writing instructors do is to use simple, familiar words -- words that mass audiences will understand. Does that mean all those hours spent in high school learning words like "egregious"1 were a waste of time?

As a budding professional writer, should you stop trying to learn new words? Is something like A Word A Day, a daily e-mail service about words, useless?

The answer, of course, is no. Your business is words, and you should have as many of them at your disposal as possible. No telling what you will want to say, and in what circumstances.

Still, it's true that you should be using simple, familiar words when you are writing for a mass audience. Talk to the audience in clear, understandable language. The point of your communication is its content, not the way in which it is communicated.

One of the foremost authorities on the English language in the late 19th and early 20th centuries was H. W. Fowler, an essayist and author of lively commentaries on the English language. One of his best books is *Modern English Usage*, and although it was published in the 1920s, it still makes delightful reading today.

In that book Fowler distinguished between "stylish" words and "working" words. "What is to be deprecated is the notion that one can improve one's style by using stylish words, or that important occasions necessarily demand important words," he wrote.

Fowler's point is that words ought to work. Writers who use a word because they think it will make them sound better (and raise their status in the eye of readers) almost inevitably fail. Such words fail on two counts. One is that the words draw attention to themselves and away from the content. And second, they often sound foppish rather than erudite.

(Are **foppish** and **erudite** working words? Look them up.)

And what's this A Word A Day? It's a daily e-mail service that gives definitions of words and some etymology. Take a look, and subscribe if you like.

1egregious (i-gree-juhs, -jee-uhs) adjective: Conspicuously bad or offensive.

[From Latin egregius, outstanding : e-, ex- + grex, greg-, herd.]
Source: A Word A Day

Precision

Precision with language is basic to the credibility of the writer. No writer can survive for very long if he or she continues to make grammatical errors to misuse the meanings of words.

Credibility is critically important for all professionals. A writer must do nothing that damages the confidence that the audience has in her ability to impart information and ideas. Grammar, punctuation and spelling errors are quick routes from respect to derision.

The next four chapters of this book are devoted to helping you increase the precision of your writing.

Efficiency

The fourth characteristic of good writing, efficiency, is a modern value, but its elevation in our understanding has had a positive impact on writing. Efficiency simply means using only the words necessary to transmit the information and ideas we have for the reader. Most eighteenth and nineteenth century writers did not practice efficiency, but we certainly remember those who did: Thomas Paine ("These are the times that try men's souls"), Thomas Jefferson (". . . all men are created equal"), Benjamin Franklin and Abraham Lincoln among them.

In the twentieth and twenty-first centuries, we have placed a high premium on time. Consequently, we do not want to waste time reading flowery prose for its own sake. Yet, many of our professions have not caught up to this truth. The legal profession is certainly a chief sinner in this regard.

Efficient writing is not necessarily equated with brevity, although that is often one of its positive outcomes. The efficient writer makes sure that every word carried some information weight, that every phase is necessary to complete the meaning. The efficient writer looks for the fat in the writing and tries to cut it out. The efficient writer is sensitive the silliness of phrases such as "at this point in time," knowing that the word "now" is more than adequate.

Efficient writing, like simple writing, is not easy to achieve. It takes time and effort. Mark Twain, a master at efficient writing, once wrote, "I didn't have time to write you a short letter, so I wrote you a long one." His point, of course, was that efficient writing requires the writer to edit and sometimes re-draft. But writers who take the time to do this show respect for their readers and keep the compact of trust that they have with them.

Many people think that the ability to write well is a talent that one either has or does not have. To some extent that may be true. But the reality is that innate talent has relatively little to do with producing clear, coherent prose. The world of literature is filled with stories of great writers struggling to get down what they have to say, composing several drafts, and editing their work endlessly. But most of us are called upon to write at a different level than the great artists of literature. In our world good writing, particularly in today's professional circles, is more about thinking and developing the right habits and techniques than about talent. Those habits can begin with a consideration of the building blocks of writing: words, sentences and paragraphs.

Terms

Sumerians	Henry Fowler	accuracy
clay tablets	invisible writing	clarity
The Epic of Gilgamesh	modesty	precision
journalism	audience	efficiency
	verbs	simplicity

Mastering the language

No one can be good at writing without mastering the basic tool – the English language. That is what we mean by precision in writing. Writing precisely means writing with an understanding of the language, following the commonly accepted rules of grammar, punctuation and spelling, and using words for their precise and accepted meanings.

Writing Lincoln's First Inaugural Address

Lincoln's second inaugural gets a great deal of attention from historians, but the circumstances of his 1861 speech made it one of the most important addresses ever given to that point in American history.

Lincoln's election had provoked widespread feelings through the South that secession was the only option left for the slave-holding states. The voices advocating a separate nation thundered loudly and in states like Alabama, Mississippi and South Carolina had overtaken any expression of moderation.

The president-elect had not spoken to the nation since his nomination because campaigning for the presidency after one received the nomination of a party was thought to be undignified. Consequently, Lincoln's words carried great import for the immediate future of the country. Different factions projected different attitudes onto the upcoming speech. Anti-slavery supporters expected Lincoln to stand up to the Southern firebrands. Moderates on all sides urged conciliation. Hard-line Southerners expected little from Lincoln that could change their minds, and many of them did not want to change their minds.

Still, the president had to try to hold the country together with this speech

He showed drafts of it to several people including **William Seward**, his chief rival for the Republican presidential nomination and now his nominee for Secretary of State. Seward suggested changes throughout, but he was most disturbed at Lincoln's ending. Seward had counseled moderation, and Lincoln's draft, he thought, was far too harsh to give moderation any hope.

Instead, he suggested this ending:

I close. We are not we must not be aliens or enemies but fellow countrymen and brethren. Although passion has strained our bonds of affection too hardly, they must not, I am sure they will not be broken. The mystic chords which proceeding from so many battle fields and so many patriot graves pass through all the hearts and all the hearths in this broad continent of ours will yet again harmonize their ancient music when breathed upon by the guardian angel of the nation.

Lincoln took those words and ideas and made them his own:

I am loth to close. We are not enemies, but friends. We must not be enemies. Though passion may have strained it must not break our bonds of affection. The mystic chords of memory, stretching from every battle-field, and patriot grave, to every living heart and hearthstone, all over this broad land, will yet swell the chorus of the Union, when again touched, as surely they will be, by the better angels of our nature.

Lincoln's sharp thinking and succinct writing took Seward's good words and turned them into what Doris Kerns Goodwin calls "powerful poetry."

The words did not, unfortunately, prevent disunion and four years of bloody battles. But when that was done, they gave voice to the enduring sentiment of American unity.

(Much of the information above comes from Doris Kerns Goodwin, Team of Rivals, Simon and Schuster, 2006.)

Exciting grammar

What could be duller than learning the rules of grammar?

Students across the decades have recoiled at learning the dictates of grammar, spelling and punctuation. Learning how to use the rules is not intellectually beyond them, but they often look upon grammar as a means of stifling their creativity or simply imposing rules unnecessarily on their writing efforts. "If someone can understand what I have written," they argue, "then why should I worry too much about following the rules."

These resisters – and unfortunately there are professional teachers among them – have failed to see that grammar brings an order to the use of the language that is good for both writers and readers. They do not understand that punctuation rules, properly used, can help a reader through a piece of prose and can enhance its meaning. Take the phrase "God save the Queen," for instance. Watch how the meaning changes – sometimes subtly, sometimes considerably – when we change the punctuation:

God save the Queen.

God, save the Queen.

God. Save the Queen.

God, save the Queen?

God save the Queen!

God! Save the Queen.

A thorough knowledge of the rules of grammar and punctuation and an application of those rules to our writing is another way in which writers can become modest – a concept introduced just a few paragraphs ago. If we use proper grammar and punctuation in our writing, it becomes a non-issue with our readers. All of us have to have some sensitivity to good grammar and punctuation; that is, as readers, if rules are broken we are likely to notice. And the act of noticing takes away from the content of the writing. Good writers try to avoid these distractions and keep the focus on their content.

Most of all, what grammar-resisters miss is the power of the language to change lives. Writing changes nations, and it changes individuals. It imbues people with ideas and reasons to act. It alters the course of history.

Take a look at the essay later in this book on the effect that Thomas Paine's *American Crisis* had on the tattered and torn American army of George Washington in December 1776. Paine's writing put into words the feelings that many of those soldiers had about what they were doing. Paine articulated their ideas with words so simple and clear – so well formed and error-free – that Washington himself credited Paine with saving the army, boosting its moral, and reviving it to score an astonishing victory over the British forces a few days later.

Observance of the rules of English is far from a nuisance. It's a necessity.

And properly done, it can be powerful.

Words

Good writers must pay attention to their words. One of the strengths of English is that it possesses so many words. The language offers us a great variety of ways in which to express our information and ideas, and it allows us to be subtle and precise in our descriptions. We often fail to take advantage of that strength, however, and we often sling words around without understanding their precise definitions.

Worse, we sometimes use words to dilute meaning rather than condense it, to confuse readers rather than inform them. We create words and phrases that we hope will elevate our importance but do little to increase the understanding of our readers. Truly good writers – the ones who care about their craft and their readers – try to avoid these nefarious schemes.

English is a language rich in words. One estimate is that it has more than 500,000 words – compared to fewer than 200,000 for German and 100,000 for French. English has always been a dynamic language, but never more so than today. New words are constantly being added to the language, while other words are changing mean or dropping out of use altogether.

Most of us know between one and two percent of the language. That is, we can recognize between 5,000 and 10,000 words. (One scholarly estimate of William Shakespeare's vocabulary is that he used some 30,000 words in his plays and poetry.) We tend to use far fewer words than we actually know, if for no other reason that we never encounter a cause to use them.

But words are certainly important to the good writer, and having a large vocabulary adds to the arsenal that a writer can use in communicating with a reader. More important than knowing words, however, is the ability to understand the subtleties of their use. For instance, the phrase "cease and desist" is popular in legal circles, and at first glance it sounds redundant. Don't they mean the same thing? Not exactly. Cease means to stop. Desist means, in street language, "back off" or "don't even think about it." Should they both, then, be used? Not necessarily. In many instances, the simple word "stop" will do. But sometimes, we may want to lay emphasis and add meaning, and in those instances both words may be employed.

Good writers are sensitive to the nuances of meaning that words have and to the ways that people understand them. That is why one of the inevitable pieces of advice you will find in any book or article that advises on improvement of writing (including this one) is to read widely. But read smartly. Take note of how writers use the language, what words they employ and how they construct their sentences. Good writers read analytically, making judgments about what they have read and consciously using those judgments to improve their own writing.

ESSAY: William Shakespeare

The Bard is not highly popular with college students these days. In fact, he has rarely been popular, although his genius is universally recognized.

You might go to one of his plays (because it's required or you're getting extra credit), but you'd rather be buried in a toxic waste dump than be caught reading his stuff.

It's obscure, opaque, convoluted.

And **loquacious** (look it up).

Words, words, words. That's what you get with Shakespeare. Lots and lots of words. He goes on and on, sometimes about the smallest point. There's plenty of action in his plays, but he slows it down with all the words.

With a writing style like that, of course, he would never make it in a high school or collegiate media writing course. He'd flunk, hands down. And particularly in the broadcast writing section. Tell him to write a 30-second broadcast news story, and he would go on for five minutes and never make it to the "cause" part of dramatic unity.

Maybe.

Compared to Shakespeare's extensive vocabulary, about 30,000 words, the well-educated person of today knows about 15,000. Most of us use far fewer than that.

But the ones we do use, particularly in our everyday speech -- well, many of those originated with Shakespeare. Consider the following expressions:

more in sorrow than in anger   fool's paradise

vanished into thin air   bag and baggage

refused to budge   high time

played fast and loose   game is up

tower of strength   truth will out

hoodwinked   if the truth were known

fair play   send him packing

cold comfort   laughing stock

too much of a good thing

The list could go on and on. (By the way, it comes from English journalist Bernard Levin's book **Enthusiasms**.) These expressions -- many of which are now considered clichés -- first appeared in Shakespeare's work. They weren't clichés when he wrote them, of course. They were fresh expressions, uses and combinations of words that no one had ever thought of before.

And they were so good that people remembered them and kept using them.

So, when Will Shakespeare, student number 00023456, signs up for a media writing course, his instructor will have some work to do. The instructor may have to reign him in a bit, tell him he's got to stick to the 30-second time limit for his broadcast news stories.

But, if the instructor smart, he or she listen very closely to what he has to say and the way he says it. Everyone in the class might learn a thing or two.

Sentences

While words are the building blocks for writers, they are not in themselves sufficient for the writer to do his or her work. Words do not construct meaning, just as shingles do not make a roof. The shingles must be put onto some sheeting and felt. So, too, words need a frame or structure. That structure is, of course, the sentence.

The construction of a sentence is what the writer does, and it is one of the most complex tasks that the human mind undertakes. A simple sentence involves thousands of factors that would make complex mathematical calculations look like simple addition and subtraction by comparison. The purpose here is not to dissect this process. Most of us learn how to construct sentences at an early age by listening and imitating, and our sophistication in doing so grows as we mature.

But writing is different from speaking. With writing we have to slow our brains down to give our words and their combinations more consideration. We have to remind ourselves of things that as speakers we would not be concerned about. One of those things is that English is made up of eight parts of speech: nouns, pronouns, verbs, adverbs, adjectives, conjunction, prepositions and interjections. We also know that we will probably not be using all eight parts of speech in the sentence we are about to construct, but we will almost certainly be using two of the following three: a noun or a pronoun and a verb.

At this point, we must remember the concept of order (or syntax). Like most languages, English has a standard but not rigid order for words: A noun that is the subject of a sentence usually comes before the verb of the sentence; and adjectives usually precede the nouns they modify. Consequently, we can reduce sentence construction to a simple concept:

Noun or pronoun (or subject) – verb (predicate).

Such a construction is known to us from our childhood, but it often helps improve our writing if we remind ourselves as to how sentences begin.

A sentence, in its basic form, is a set of words containing a subject (noun or pronoun) and a verb that expresses a complete thought. The words "Going to the store" is not a complete thought; it does not give us enough information to form a picture that we can share with the writer. The words "He is going to the store" is a complete thought. The writer of this sentence has written something that we can understand much as the writer meant for us to.

Once we remind ourselves of the basic structure of a sentence, we can then remember that standard English offers us a variety of sentence structures that we can use in our writing. This is a good thing because English and our writing would be awfully dull if every sentence we wrote were only subject-verb. In fact, one of the hallmarks of good writing is the mixture of various sentence lengths and structures. Good writers consciously try to use short, medium and long sentences (although, generally, they do not let sentences become too long). They also consciously use the four basic types of sentence structures: simple, compound, complex, and compound-complex.

A **simple sentence** confines itself to a subject and a single verb. The example we used above will suffice:

He is going to the store.

A **compound sentence** puts two sentences (often referred to as independent clauses) together with either a comma and coordinating conjunction or a semicolon:

He is going to the store, and he will come back.

In this case, "and" is the coordinating conjunction. Grammatically, you would be correct in writing the following: He is going to the store; he will come back. However, it would not be correct to write: He is going to the store, he will come back. This is a comma splice or run-on sentence and is a serious grammatical error.

A **complex sentence** is one that has an independent clause (He is going to the store) and a dependent clause. A dependent (sometimes called subordinate) clause contains a subject and a verb but does not itself express a complete thought. This sentence is an example of a complex sentence:

He is going to the store after he takes a nap.

The words "after he takes a nap" do not express a complete thought and cannot stand alone as a sentence.

A compound-complex sentence is a compound sentence that also contains a dependent clause.

He is going to the store after he takes his nap, and he will come back.

Note that this type of sentence still requires a comma and a coordinating conjunction to be grammatically correct.

Nothing in this section discusses the content of writing – the actual information and ideas that you may want to write about. That was deliberate. Much of the rest of this book is devoted to that. Here, we simply want you to concentrate on the technical side of writing.

Paragraphs

With coherent, grammatically correct sentences, a writer forms paragraphs. Paragraphs are collections of sentences (usually more than one sentence, but not always) whose content connects them with each other. Paragraphs serve two purposes. One is that they help the writer organize thoughts and information. The second is that they help the reader get through a piece of writing with visual cues. A new paragraph gives the reader a small visual break in the text and signals the reader that a new set of sentences is about to begin.

Paragraphs should be neither too short nor too long. Most writing texts advise against one-sentence paragraphs, arguing that a single sentence does not provide enough development for the reader. One exception to the no-one-sentence-paragraph is in journalism where writers are advised to use short paragraphs because columns of type are so narrow that readers need the visual breaks that paragraphs offer.

A greater danger from beginning writers in other fields, however, is paragraphs that run too long. Many young writers do not get into the habit of paragraphing properly and consequently are likely to let their paragraphs run too long – sometimes page after page with no new paragraphs at all. The art of paragraphing is one that every good writer must cultivate. It involves some serious thinking about the writing, often as the composition is in progress. The writer must group his or her thoughts into a coherent set that will begin and end at a reasonable length.

Paragraphing is part of the rhythm of writing that requires some study and much practice. As with many other aspects of writing, there is no substitute for analytical reading in learning how to paragraph. Seeing how good writers paragraph is vital to anyone learning how to write well.

One other aspect of paragraphing should be mentioned: transitions. Paragraphs should be tied together in a logical and coherent fashion. Otherwise, the writing will be disjointed and difficult for the reader to follow. Ideally, writing should flow from one sentence to another, one paragraph to the next. But to make this seem natural requires a deliberate act on the part of the writer. That is why transitional devices are so important to the writer and should be studied and used carefully. Transitions help the writer lead the reader on through a pattern of thought or logic that the writer establishes.

Start writing

One of the most difficult parts of the writing process is getting started. Faced with the empty sheet of paper or the blank screen, many people cringe, even experienced professionals. Novelist Ernest Hemingway once wrote that he would sharpen twenty pencils every morning just as a way of avoiding the beginning of the writing process.

As a young adult novelist Will Hobbs began writing fulltime at home by himself while his wife was working in real estate. To get himself started he used to start an animated model of a dinosaur. He would wind it up and place it on one side of his desk. His goal was to be started writing by the time the model made it to the other side of his desk.

Writers must choose, out of thousands of possibilities, those first few words that will begin the process, and that choice is rarely easy. Many writers fear sounding inane, boring or clichéd with their first words, and unfortunately those fears often are justified.

So how do you get started?

Coming to the writing process fully prepared makes starting the process a bit easier. That means gathering all of the material that you will need for your writing session. Any notes, information or other material that you will need should be readily at hand.

Understanding the form in which you are writing also helps in getting started. Are you writing a letter, a note, a memo, a report, an essay, a news article or what? The form often dictates how a piece of writing should begin. There may be some obligatory words that the writer must use to start the form (such as "Dear Mr. Smith" for a letter). Understanding the form of writing also helps the writer see the whole piece from beginning to end and certainly can be a guide to organizing the material to be written.

Another technique for getting the writing process going is to think like a journalist. In writing a news story, a journalist has to decide what is the most important piece of information that must be related to the reader – the score of the game, the outcome of a city council vote, the effects of a fire, etc. Journalists have to put their information into a descending order of importance, starting with the most important or interesting and going to the least important or interesting. As you begin writing, think about the most important thing you have to say to your readers.

The value of making notes and outlines cannot be overemphasized in the writing process. An outline, no matter how sparse, can give the writer a view of the piece as a whole and can serve as a guide through the information once the writing process begins. A good outline can ready the brain for the process of writing. Outlines should be in any form that makes the writer comfortable and the writing process easier. Some people prefer long, elaborate outlines; others use just a few words. Whatever the case, an outline can serve as a time-saving aide to the writer. An outline also can be a key to revision, to see what you have actually written and then, as a result of what the outline tells you, how you need to revise.

ESSAY: The audacity of hope for Barack Obama, the writer

It was with plenty of audacity and no small amount of hope that Barack Obama sat down in the early 1990s to write his life story.

He had just turned 30 in 1991 and could reasonably assume that much was ahead of him -- an assumption that would be true, of course -- but he also knew that his life to that point had been like no one else's whom he knew:

- The son of a white mother from Kansas and an African father from Kenya;

- Raised in Indonesia, Africa and Hawaii;

- Intellectually brilliant, confirmed by the fact that he was editor of the Harvard Law Review.

Obama's defining experience to that point had been his relationship with his father, with him he had lost touch early in life and then re-established contact. Shortly after that, however, his father died, and Obama traveled to Kenya to find out more about the man. There, many of the images he had of his father are shattered. He finds that his father had slid from being a brilliant and respected academic to a drunk and an object of pity.

The small amount of fame that Obama achieved as being the first black editor of the Harvard Law Review netted him a call from a literary agent, a book proposal and a publisher. His first idea was to write about race relations, but that didn't suit him and where he was, according to <u>an article about the book</u> by Janny Scott published by the New York Times.

That journey of discovery through the images he had of his father is what he decided he had to tackle. What he produced was **Dreams From My Father.**

He did so with confidence and flair -- even audacity -- using composite characters, invented dialogue, out-of-sequence events and a variety of literary techniques. He has since come under some criticism for his account. Inquiring journalists and political opposition researchers say things didn't happen the way he said they happened.

But there is one fact that no one disputes. Obama **wrote** his own book.

He struggled with sentences, phrasing and structure. He edited, rewrote and rethought.

The words are his and his alone. He didn't pay a ghostwriter or take on some partner to do the literary heavy-lifting. The writing is his creation. In this age of spin and carefully calibrated public pronouncements, getting an unobstructed look into the mind of a prominent political figure does not happen very often.

Questions for discussion

1. What is the best environment for you to write in – a quiet room, a radio or MP3 playing, food at hand, etc.? Do you always try to create that environment for your writing?

2. Select a short passage from one of your favorite pieces of prose. Examine the writing rather than the content. Does it contain the four qualities of good writing that the author identifies: accuracy, clarity, precision and efficiency?

3. The author makes some bold statements about the value and process of writing. Is there anything in this chapter with which you disagree? Why?

4. Based on what the author has said in this chapter, how do you think you can improve your writing? What is your biggest weakness? What is your strength as a writer?

5. Who are your audences? What are their expectations?

6. Why do you think the author put so much emphasis on understanding the sentence in this chapter?

7. One of the things the author tells his writing students is that they should not write anything unless they mean to change the lives of those who read it. What do you think about this statement? Do you agree?

Word choice quiz 1

Select the correct word for the following sentences.

She has _____ books than he does.33
less
fewer
Use "fewer" with countable items. Use "less" with amounts or things not countable.

Mary works _____ with John.
well
good˘
"Good" is an adjective and "well" is an adverb except when referring to health.

Jason named his pet _____ Mary Ann.
peacock
peahen
Peacocks are male; peahens are female, and peafowl are both.

Greg doesn't practice _____ he should.
as
like˘
"As" is used to introduce clauses; "like" is a preposition and requires an object.

General Hartley ordered his men to fire the _____ .
canon
cannon
A "cannon" is a weapon; a canon is a law or rule.

The boy was able to _____ the kidnapper.
elude
allude
"Elude," which means to escape from, is the correct choice. "Allude" means to refer to or mention.

"_____ there?" the child asked.
Whose
Who's
"Who's" is the contraction of who is, therefore it is the correct choice. "Whose" is the possessive form of who.

She has _____ books than he does.
less
Fewer
Use "fewer" with countable items; use "less" with amounts or things not countable.

"_____ the thought that counts," she said.
Its
It's

33

"It's" is the contraction of it is and is the correct choice in this example. "Its" is the possessive form of the word it.

Julia Child, noted _____, appeared on television many times.
gourmet
gourmand
"Gourmet" is a judge of fine food; "gourmand" is a glutton

The rain showers will continue to ___ through the weekend.
pore
pour
"Pour" is to flow in a continous stream; "pore" is to gaze intently

The FCC is currently deciding whether a record industry _____ is needed.
censer
censor
"Censor" is to prohibit, restrict; as a noun, it means prohibitor. "Censer" is an incense burner container

The committee is debating whether to spend the money _____ putting it in another fund.
versus
verses
"Versus" means to go against or abberate; "verses" are lines of poetry.

The inspector promised to keep him _____ of the situation.
appraised
apprised
"Apprise" means to inform; "appraise" means to give place a value on something.

The _____ goal is to establish open lines of communication.
principle
principal
"Principle" is a basic rule or guiding truth. "Principal" is a dominant or primary thing, as in the above example. "Principle" is a noun, while "principal" may be an adjective or a noun

Word choice quiz 2

Does your tone _____ that he can't be responsible?
imply
infer
"Imply" means to suggest or indicate; "infer" means to draw a conclusion from.

The smoke had an eerie _____ on the play's set.
affect
effect
"Effect" is a change or result; "affect" is always a verb that means to pretend to feel or be, to like and display or to produce an effect.

Mom placed the vase on the _____.
mantel
mantle
A "mantel" is a shelf, and a "mantle" is a cloak.

The diamond weighed two _____.
carats
karats
"Carats" are used to measure weight of precious stones. "Karats" measure the ratio of gold to the mixed alloy.

Jan's mistake was the _____ cause.
principle
principal
"Principal" means someone or something first in rank, authority, or importance. "Principle" means a fundamental truth, law or doctrine.

The total in attendance was _____ 100.
over
more than
"Over" and "under" are best used for spatial relationships. When using figures, more than and less than are better choices.

The student gave a(n) _____ report of her findings.
verbal
oral
"Oral" is used when the mouth is central to the idea, as in this case. "Verbal" may refer to spoken or written words.

Montgomery is Alabama's state _____.
capitol
capital
"Capital" refers to a seat of government. A "capitol" is the building in which a legislature sits. "Capital" is the correct answer.

Jim is exhausted and needs to _____ down.
lie
lay
"Lie" is a state of being, while "lay" is the action work. "Lay" needs an object to be used correctly. "Lie" is the correct choice.

Charles Manson received a life sentence for the _____ murders he ordered.
grizzly
grisly

"Grisly" means horrifying. "Grizzly" is bearish.

The astronauts offered their final words of _____ before takeoff.
goodbye
goodby
The proper spelling is "goodbye," not "goodby. "

During the Civil War, Richmond was _____ by Union bombardment.‴
ravaged
ravished
To "ravage" is to wreak great destruction; to "ravish" is to abduct, rape, or carry away with emotion. Buildings and towns cannot be ravished.

Smith will be staying in the Royal Dutch _____ .
suite
suits
"Suite" refers to a set of rooms & furniture; "suits" refers to clothes, cards or law suits.

The poll showed that the phrase "U.S. defense system" _____ destruction and death.
denotes
connotes
"Denotes" implies a specific meaning; "connotes" means to suggest or imply.

The candidate argued for a more _____ distribution of wealth in this nation.
equal
equitable
"Equal" is an adjective that has no comparatives; that is, you may not say that something is "more equal" or "less equal. " The adjective "equitable" does have comparatives. Therefore, it is the correct answer.

Terms

grammar	The Bard	simple sentence	paragraph
rules	Sentences	compound sentence	outli
English language	subject	complex sentence	
William Shakespeare	predicate	compound-complex sentence	

Tools of the Writer: Grammar

Grammar is an important part of the writer's toolkit – like a hammer and saw to a carpenter. The professional writer has to know how to use the tools.

When the rules didn't matter

Linguistically, eighteenth century England resembled the mythic American Wild West. What rules there were could be broken at will. Words were spelled in whatever way a writer chose to spell them. Grammar was what sounded good to the creator of the word. Punctuation had no standard.

But the English mind was collectively flourishing. Literature, some of which we now consider great and timeless, was being produced. Scientists were making huge strides and beginning to affect the lives of the population. Many were looking to the future as representing a better life for themselves, their children and their grandchildren.

Yet, many also looked at the state of the English language and despaired. How could the wonderful things that England was producing be preserved with a language so wild and chaotic? If every Tom, Dick and Harry could come along and change any word, any spelling and any punctuation point without penalty, how could one generation know or read what the previous generation had written.

The despair of these critics rose as they thought about how those on the European continent had begun to tame their languages. The Italians had a dictionary approved by an academy of scholars that had purged the vulgarities of the language and had laid out its rules and regulations. And the French – the French! – had established the Académie Francaise with a chart that directed it "to give definite rules to our language, and to render it pure" so that it could accommodate the arts and sciences. Others in England looked with envy on the orderliness of Latin and Greek and how simple and straightforward they seemed compared with what was happening in England.

Chief among those who decried the state of the language and called for a set of rules for English was Jonathan Swift, author of *Gulliver's Travels*. Swift wrote essays and letters cogently outlining the problems that English was having and the consequences of doing nothing about it. "But what I have most at Heart is," he wrote, "that some Method should be thought on for ascertaining and fixing out language for ever, after such Alterations are made in it that shall be thought requisite. For I am of the Opinion, that it is better a Language should not be thought wholly perfect, than that it should be perpetually changing. . . ."

Swift's ideas, fortunately, were not shared by everyone. Yes, the language needed some order but not rules and regulations that were immutable. Like life itself, the language was dynamic and changing, responding to new knowledge, ideas, experiences and situations. The hope that Swift and other had of an immutable and unchanging language was like the elixir that would offer eternal youth, wrote Samuel Johnson.

> *"When we see men grow old and die at a certain, one after another, century after century, we laugh at the elixir that promises to prolong life to a thousand years; and with equal justice may the lexicographer be derided, who being able to produce no example of a nation that has preserved their (sic) words and phrases from mutability, shall imagine that his dictionary can embalm his language, and secure it from corruption and decay, that it is within his power to change sublunary nature, and clear the world at once from folly, vanity, and affectation."*

Johnson, of course, was more than a critic. He knew that the English of his time needed a guide, not a dictator, and he set out to produce that guide – with monumental results.

In 1746, he contracted with a London publisher to produce a dictionary of English words. It was not the first such effort that English speakers had undertaken, but it turned out to be the most profound and influential.

Johnson labored for nine years on his dictionary. He rented space at 17 Gough Square in the heart of London and hired several assistants. He borrowed books from everyone he knew and set about finding passages of previous writings that included the words he wanted to define. It was the way these words had been used, not the way Johnson wanted them used, that guided him in formulating his definitions. Johnson could not help using his own wit, however, and sometimes that wit was aimed directly at himself:

He defined **lexicographer** as "a writer of dictionaries, a harmless drudge."

He launched a small arrow at the Scots with his definition of **oats**: "a grain, which in England is generally given to horses, but in Scotland supports the population."

He got in a jab at politicians and bureaucrats when he wrote of **pensions** as "an allowance made to anyone without an equivalent. In England it is generally understood to mean pay given to state hireling for treason to his country."

But these witticisms are the exceptions. The rule in Johnson's dictionary was clear, precise definitions with passages from literature to back them up. The book contained 43,000 definitions with more than 114,000 literary entries as support. (If Johnson had worked six days a week for nine years, that would mean that, on average, he would have produced 16 definitions with three supporting passages every day.) Johnson had single-handedly shown the world how English could evolve, how it could be stable yet dynamic, how it could be used to express the ancient and the new. Johnson imposed his own order on the language. It was not the order of immutability but the gentle guidance of a master, one who directs but does not dictate.

The wisdom of Johnson's approach is evident today. English is the closest thing we have to a universally accepted language. It has a half million words and grows daily. It has been adapted in almost every corner of the globe. French, once the international language of diplomacy, has only about 100,000 words and has been overtaken by Spanish as the preferred second language of many English speakers. French must borrow many words from English (le weekend) just to keep up, and getting them accepted by the Académie Francaise is not easy.

The use of English is not without rules, as every school child knows. One must learn to writer "properly" (and speak "properly") in order to be considered well educated. So it should be. Samuel Johnson and others who have thought seriously about the language have never advocated complete anarchy in its use. Standards for word order, word use, grammar, punctuation and spelling are necessary for the system to work – for all of us to be able to understand what we say and what we write. Knowing the commonly accepted standards – and even knowing that those standards will inevitably change in some form during our lifetime – is the responsibility that the writer accepts.

Knowing and applying the rules

Nonsensical as they are, arguments against having rules governing the use of the language can still be heard. The fact that the language is dynamic and responsive is sometimes cited to support the uselessness of teaching the rules of grammar, punctuation and spelling. Such arguments are specious. The language does change, but important and far-reaching changes are glacial. More importantly, knowledge of grammar has practical and substantial benefits.

Knowing and applying the rules of grammar, punctuation, spelling and diction can be a great help – and a great comfort – to the writer. A knowledge of the rules and the accumulated experience of applying them make the process of writing more efficient. Such knowledge frees the writer to focus on the content of the prose the rules of the language.

Knowledge of the language can also make the writer more confident. The writing process is not easy in itself, and formulating ideas and information with words can seem daunting. The writer is constantly asking, "How can I get my point across to the reader?" If the writer believes he or she can apply the commonly accepted rules of the language, it makes writing that much easier.

Beyond simply knowing and applying the rules, however, is the fact that we as intelligent and curious beings should have some interest in the basic tools that we use to communicate. It does not take the heart of a linguist to develop this interest or to satisfy our curiosity. We should be keen observers of our world, and an important part of that world is how the language is used.

Finally, it should be acknowledged that good writers know and follow the rules of usage, but they are not slaves to those rules. Most follow the dictum of George Orwell, who said, "Break any of these rules sooner than write anything barbarous."

The system and its principles

Grammar is the basic system whereby the language is used. Various approaches and attitudes can be taken toward grammar, and they have merit. Here the approach is normative and prescriptive. This text tries to examine the commonly accepted ways of using the language and advising those conventions be followed as closely as possible. A great majority of those conventions make sense in the environment in which we communicate. Some of those conventions are being overcome by new habits of usage or growing out of date. It remains valuable for us to learn what the conventions and rules are so we can make intelligent decisions about their use.

- Standardization allows us to communicate more effectively and efficiently.

- Knowledge of those rules makes us better writer. We have more confidence in the way that we are saying things.

- People who work with the language — people like you — should care about it. They should take an active interest in its development.

- The rules — grammar, spelling, punctuation -- are dynamic rather than stagnant. They change often. Knowing grammar is not just knowing a set of rule. Rather, it is understanding how the language works and how it is used.

Media writers must keep up with the language and the way in which people are using it.

Knowledge of the rules of grammar, punctuation, spelling and style are important to your professional reputation.

Parts of speech

In English, words are used in eight different ways; we call them parts of speech, and most school children are introduced to parts of speech in their early formal language training. They are:

Nouns, words that designate people, things or ideas;

Pronouns, words that can be substituted for nouns;

Verbs, words that describe actions or state of being;

Adjectives, words that modify or describe nouns or sometimes other adjectives;

Adverbs, words that modify or describe verbs or sometimes other adverbs;

Prepositions, words that in combination with a noun (and its adjectives) or pronoun form a phrase that modifies a noun or a verb;

Conjunctions, words that tie together words, phrases or ideas in a sentence;

Interjections, words that express some strong emotion. (Interjections are sometimes not considered one of the parts of speech because their use in formal writing is fairly rare.)

Word order

Word order is a crucial part of grammar. One of the major tasks of very young children who are just learning to speak is to learn appropriate word order. Because English is a complex language and because there are so many words and so many possible combinations, this task is one of the most difficult encountered during childhood. Most of us, for better or worse, accomplish it, however. Most of what we learn is then transferred to our writing.

We learn that the basic sentence – the unit of words that we use to express our thoughts – consists of a noun followed by a verb. The verb may then be following by words or phrases that will complete the thought of the sentence, as in the following:

Jane throws the ball.

Jane is the noun and is the subject of the sentence; "throws" is the verb. In this sentence "ball" is called the object because the action of the verb is visited upon it. In most sentences, you can find a subject, verb and object in this order. (At this point, you should begin to pay attention to verbs. We will have much more to say about them in the next chapter.)

One of the important concepts in grammar is agreement, or agreement in number. One of the peculiarities of English is that it distinguishes between one and more than one of something – not just in its descriptions of objects but grammatically as well. Consequently, we refer to some words as being singular, such as "him," and other words as being plural, such as "them." Verbs have singular and plural forms also: "was" is singular, and "were" is plural. Certain word combinations, most importantly subjects and verbs, must be in agreement – that is, "agreement in number" – when used together in a sentence. "He are going to the store" is incorrect because "He" is singular, and "are" is plural. The correct version is "He is going to the store."

Another important concept for understanding grammar is that of tense. Tense is the time period referred to by the verb. Basically, a verb can be past, present or future tense. Verbs in English begin with a present tense "root" from which the other tenses are formed. Most verbs are "regular" verbs; that is, you form the past tense of the verb by adding -ed, -ied or -d to the root (act, acted; hurry, hurried; slice, sliced). Some verbs are "irregular" and past tenses are formed differently (give, given; read, read; write, wrote, written). Irregular verbs must be memorized because there is no pattern to them, and they are what give fits to those learning English as a second language. Even native English speakers sometimes get into bad habits by incorrectly using irregular verbs.

Common grammar problems

Most of the time, most people – particularly at the college level – use English according to the commonly accepted rules of grammar. They do this both in speaking and in writing. They have learned to do this for a variety of reasons: study and practice, habits, good influences, etc. They continue to be careful about their grammar for social reasons: to use improper grammar is a sign of a lack of learning or carelessness, or both.

Still, problems with grammar continue to plague many of us. These problems are sometimes subtle, but they can be devastating to those who have them in a professional and education environment.

Agreement, subject-verb

The rule is simple: Singular subjects require singular verbs, and plural subjects require plural verbs. Yet problems arise in sentences where the subject may be in question or where it is obscured by what comes immediately after it, as in the following sentence:

The cargo of vegetables and fruits were unloaded quickly.

The subject of the sentence is "cargo" not "fruits and vegetables" even though these are related to the subject.

Another problem with subject-verb agreement is the compound subject, or what may appear to be a compound subject. If two nouns or pronouns are joined by a conjunction, they would take a plural verb, such as the following:

John and Margo are going to the dance.

But other constructions may make them appear to be a compound subject when they really are not:

John, along with his friend Margo, are going to the dance.

In this sentence, the subject is simply "John," and the verb should be singular.

A few words in English appear to be singular when they are really plural. One such word is "media," and it is often misused. Media is the plural of medium, and it is incorrect to write:

The mass media is a tremendous force in today's society.

Should "media" be singular?

One of the strengths of English is its dynamic nature. Words change in their meaning – two generations ago "gay" did not mean "homosexual" – and in their usage. "Media" may be one of those words. It is commonly used as a singular noun. Should we then change the rule for this word? Or, should we stand fast with the rule?

Finally, British common usage sometimes differs with American usage in whether or not certain words take a singular or plural noun. In British usage, there are many more "collective nouns," words that refer to a group of people, that take plural verbs. For instance:

The faculty are meeting in the conference room.

In American usage, this construction is considered incorrect because the word faculty is singular despite the fact that it refers to more than one person. In British usage, however, it is quite acceptable.

Agreement, pronoun-antecedent

An antecedent is a word in a sentence to which a pronoun later in the sentence refers. Both the antecedent and pronoun should agree in number, and one of the most commonly accepted and overlooked grammatical mistakes in spoken English is the pronoun-antecedent disagreement.

After the game, the team found their bus in the parking lot.

In this sentence, the pronoun "their" is plural but refers to a singular noun "team." Consequently, the sentence is incorrect. The word "its" should be substituted for "their." While this may be common in spoken English, it is not correct in written English, and the careful writer will pay attention to this point.

Strict adherence to the rule that singular antecedents must have singular pronouns can lead to some awkward constructions. For instance, we have a tendency to say or write:

Everyone who is ready can begin their test.

It might be acceptable to say it that way; in fact, in many circles it might be preferable. Writing that, however, is still incorrect. Properly, the sentence above should be:

Everyone who is ready can begin his or her test.

Often this problem can be avoided by changing the subject to a word that is plural. Note that in this example, the object ("tests") should be changed, too.

All who are ready can begin their tests.

The writer who uses pronouns and antecedents correctly shows that he or she is both knowledgeable and careful.

Sentence fragments

Sentences require both a subject and a verb that work together to make a complete thought. In writing we sometimes get so involved in our ideas and information that we neglect one of those two elements in constructing a sentence.

Going to the store on a bright, sunny day with a song in his heart and Rachel on his mind.

John, the bright young man who would not be deterred from taking some of the most difficult courses in the curriculum.

Because she was injured badly in the war and could not use both of her legs well which prevented her from entering the race.

Sentence fragments can usually be avoided, or discovered, with a careful reading of our writing. They can also be avoided if we would get into the habit of writing in shorter sentences and not trying to pack too much information or too many ideas before the periods.

That, which, and who

Should a subordinate clause in a sentence begin with "that," "which," or "who"? The answer to that lies, in part, in what roll the subordinate clause plays in the sentence. A subordinate clause that is necessary for the reader to understand what the writer is saying is called an essential or restrictive clause. It should begin with the pronoun "that," as in the following:

The amendment to the U.S. Constitution that grants us freedom of speech and assembly also gives us the right to worship freely.

The subordinate clause in this sentence is "that grants us freedom of speech and assembly," and it is necessary for the reader to understand the meaning of the sentence. As such, it should be introduced with "that," and it should not be set off from the rest of the sentence with commas.

A subordinate clause that is not necessary to the meaning of the sentence is called a non-essential or a non-restrictive clause. It should be set off from the rest of the sentence with commas, and it should begin with "which," as in the following:

The horse, which is owned by a group of investors, won the race easily.

Deciding whether or not a clause is necessary to the meaning of a sentence is the tricky part of this problem. Once the writer has decided, however, it is a fairly straightforward matter as to which pronoun, that or which, should be used.

The consideration about that or which can be set aside when people – not objects or ideas – are being referred to by a subordinate clause. In those cases, the appropriate pronoun to use is "who" rather than "that" or "which." Consequently, it would be incorrect to write:

The girl that was just here stole my trousers.

Correctly written, the sentence is:

The girl who was just here stole my trousers.

Notice that "who was just here" is treated as an essential clause and is not set off from the sentence by commas. Here is an example of a sentence where "who" is used in a non-restrictive clause:

John, who was my roommate last year, won the race by more than two yards.

The concept of essential and non-essential clauses is one that a careful writer will pay a good deal of attention to and in so doing, avoid grammatical and punctuation mistakes.

Dangling participles

Introductory phrases or clauses – that is, those that come at the beginning of a sentence – should refer to or modify the subject of the sentence. If they do not, they are known as "dangling participles" or "dangling phrases," and they can make for some amusing and problematic writing:

Cluttered and messy, my boyfriend could not keep his room straight.

After driving all night, my dog appeared well rested because he slept in the back seat of the car.

These sentences show that the writers were interrupted in their thoughts while composing the sentences and that they did not recognize the problems during the editing process.

Some critics of the grammar police point to the strictures on dangling participles and argue, in effect, "If you can understand what the writer meant, so what if the participle dangles! Who cares?"

Well, maybe.

The problem with that thinking – particularly if one wants to be a professional writer – is that readers DO care. The careful reader notices these things and generally is very forgiving on the writer who commits grammatical sins.

Active and passive voice

Most texts on good writing, including this one, advise that writers should use the active voice rather than the passive voice. What are they talking about? Not only do verbs have a tense, but they can also have a "voice." Voice refers to the way in which the verb is used to construct the sentence. Active voice means that the subject of the sentence is the "doer" or perpetrator of the action:

Mary hurled the javelin for a new school record.

The passive voice uses a "helping verb" and throws the action onto the object or predicate rather than the subject:

The javelin was hurled by Mary for a new school record.

Most writing instructors agree that in most cases, writers should try to use the active rather than passive voice. It is more direct and efficient, and it takes greater advantage of strong, descriptive verbs, such as the one used in the example above.

A more insidious use of the passive voice is when it obscures the subject or allows the subject to evade responsibility for the action, as in the following:

It was decided that she should not receive tenure.

The question that immediately arises from this sentence is, "Who decided that?" The writer who constructs a sentence like that is not giving the reader all of the information the reader should have.

The passive voice cannot and should not be avoided all the time. There are occasions when the passive voice is useful and necessary to convey information correct and give the proper emphasis. For instance:

The accident victims were taken to the hospital by an ambulance.

We could write that sentence as, "An ambulance took the accident victims to the hospital" to avoid the passive voice, but that would be putting the emphasis of the sentence on the ambulance rather than the victims. Using the passive voice, however, should always give the careful writer pause and should raise the question, "Is the passive voice in this instance really necessary?" If the answer is no, the writer should rewrite the sentence to use the active voice.

Agreement quiz 1

None of the members of the first team are playing in the fourth quarter.
a. correct
* b. incorrect

49

Words such as none, anyone, everybody, each, either, neither and one are singular when used as subjects in a sentence. In this case, none is the subject of the sentence, not members. The verb "are" is incorrect; it should be "is."

The family was gathering from around the country for the funeral.
a. correct
* b. incorrect
The noun family is a collective noun. Collective nouns refer to a group of things or people as a unit. Some other examples of such words are class, committee, team, number, majority, group, herd and jury. When these words are used as subjects and denote the unit as a whole, they are singular and take singular verbs.

Today's news media is generally considered to be politically liberal.
a. correct
* b. incorrect
Some words retain their Latin origins. "Media" is such a word. "Data" is another word of this kind. Although they are often used as singular nouns, they are plural and should be used with plural verbs. "Media" is plural for "medium," and the verb should be "are" rather than "is."

Rachel, despite everyone's best efforts, was not able to pass the test.
* a. correct
b. incorrect
The subject of the sentence is Rachel, not efforts.

Present at the ceremony was the big league pitcher Mike O'Kelley and his brother Robert.
a. correct
* b. incorrect
This sentence has a compound subject - Mike O'Kelley and Robert. Compound subjects joined by the conjunction "and" usually take plural verbs. The verb should be "were" rather than "was." Don't be fooled by the fact that the subject comes after the verb rather than before it.

Thelma and Louise, the movie, make some telling points about women in our society.
a. correct
* b. incorrect
Titles of books, movies and other works should be treated as singular nouns even though they may be plural in form. In this case Thelma and Louise is the title of the move and should be treated as a singular noun. The verb should be "makes" instead of "make."

Everyone, even the smartest ones among us, has a bad day now and then.
* a. correct
b. incorrect

Words such as everyone, none, anyone, everybody, each, either, neither and one are singular when used as subjects in a sentence. Don't be fooled by the plural nouns in the parenthetical phrase that follows the subject.

Either her doctor or her lawyer has a standing appointment to visit her every morning.
a. correct
b. incorrect
Compound subjects joined by the conjunction "or" or in the constructions "either ... or" and "neither ... nor" usually take singular verbs.
Both Mary and Joan play the piano with ease and grace.
* a. correct
b. incorrect
This sentence has a compound subject that is joined by the conjunction "and." The subject thus requires a plural verb.

Agreement quiz 2

Either of the two boys have the ability to make the team.
a. correct
* b. incorrect
Words such as none, anyone, everybody, each, either, neither and one are singular when used as subjects in a sentence. In this case, either is the subject of the sentence, not boys. The verb "have" is incorrect; it should be "has."

The committee members meet once a month to try to determine the policies of the organization.
* a. correct
b. incorrect
This sentence has a plural subject, members, and, therefore, it must take the plural form of the verb. Remember that unlike most nouns, most verbs taken their plural form by adding an "s."

The babies in the nursery, and one in particular, was crying for some attention.
a. correct
* b. incorrect
The subject in this sentence is babies, but the verb, was, is singular. The verb should be were.

The politics of the committee were such that no one could be elected chair of the group.
* a. correct
b. incorrect
Some words can be either singular or plural depending on their context. The writer must decide which is the proper use. Politics is one of those words. Here the writer is referring to a variety of situations that constitute the workings of the group.

A bizarre series of incidents has surrounded that old house lately.
a. correct
* b. incorrect
Despite its plural form, the word "series" is a singular noun. The verb should be "has" rather than "have."

The president jogged by the group of tourists who were gaping out the window of the bus.
* a. correct
b. incorrect
In this sentence, the phrase "who were gaping out the window of the bus" is a dependent clause, but it contains the subject "who." The question is, to what does the "who" refer - the "group" or the "tourists." In this case, it is the "tourists;" consequently, the "who" should take a plural verb.

A wide variety of strategic reasons have been used to explain Napoleon's defeat at Waterloo.
a. correct
* b. incorrect
The subject of this sentence is "variety," a singular noun. The verb should also be singular - "has," rather than "have."

Incidents of alcohol abuse account for many traffic fatalities each year.
* a. correct
b. incorrect
The subject of this sentence, "Incidents," requires the plural form of the verb, "account."

Few of the senators were on hand for the vote.
* a. correct
b. incorrect
The word "few," even though singular in appearance, is considered a plural and should take a plural verb. Few refers to the individuals in a group rather than to a group itself.

The most resilient among the war's survivors were the children.
* a. correct
b. incorrect
In this sentence "resilient" is an adjective that appears to be replacing some noun - possibly "survivors" - as the subject of the sentence. Whatever the noun, it is obviously plural, and consequently, the verb should also be plural.

Restrictive and non-restrictive clauses quiz 1

Are the clauses underlined in these sentences restrictive or non-restrictive?
The ring <u>that she really liked</u> had been sold by the store by the time she got back there.
* Restrictive
Non-restrictive
The clause "that she really liked" is a restrictive or essential clause. It is necessary to the meaning of the sentence.

The district, <u>which he represented</u>, was redrawn after the last census.
Restrictive
* Non-restrictive
The clause is not essential because it is not necessary to the understanding of the sentence, even though it does add some information.

The best-selling novel <u>The Bridges of Madison County</u> brought its author much unexpected fame and fortune.
* Restrictive
Non-restrictive
The question here is how necessary is the title of the novel to the understanding of the sentence. It is necessary because the sentence is not talking about all or any best-selling novel. If it were, the title would be set off by commas.

The painting, <u>framed and hanging in the back of the gallery</u>, was priced at more than $10,000.
Restrictive
* Non-restrictive
The phrase adds information but is not essential to the meaning of the sentence.

The cannon explosions, <u>which began just after midnight</u>, lasted for more than three hours.
Restrictive
* Non-restrictive
This clause is not necessary for the reader to understand the meaning of the sentence. One tipoff for this clause being non-essential is that it is set off from the rest of the sentence by commas. Another is that it is introduced by the pronoun "which."

A boy <u>whom I hired last week</u> did not show up for work today.
* Restrictive
Non-restrictive
Read this sentence without the underlined clause. It doesn't tell the reader very much. The writer wants the reader to know specifically whom he is talking about, and so it restricts the mean of "boy.".

We watched the entire movie, <u>which was more than three hours long</u>.

Restrictive
* Non-restrictive
This clause adds information but is not essential for the meaning of the sentence.

The death penalty, <u>a punishment that most other countries have abolished</u>, was reinstated by the Supreme Court in 1976.
Restrictive
* Non-restrictive
This one is a little confusing. The appositive phrase "a punishment that most other countries have abolished" is non-essential. Within that phrase, however, is a clause that is essential. The sentence would not sound right without it.

He gave his tickets to the man <u>who was standing by the door</u>.
* Restrictive
Non-restrictive
The lack of a comma separating this clause from the rest of the sentence indicates that it is an essential clause and cannot be removed from the sentence.

The Air Force Band, <u>which we heard in concert three years ago</u>, played at the funeral of the former secretary of defense.
Restrictive
* Non-restrictive
Notice that the pronoun "which" introduces this non-essential clause.

Terms

grammar	parts of speech	fragment
Academie Francaise	medium, media	restrictive clause
Jonathan Swift	word order	non-restrictive clause
Samuel Johnson	agreement	subordinate clause
active voice	dangling participle	independent clause
passive voice	pronoun-antecedent	

Tools of the Writer: Punctuation

Punctuation can clutter a sentence and confuse the reader, or it can make the sentence crystal clear. Proper and discreet use of punctuation is another powerful tool in the hands of a good writer. A well-punctuated sentence can help the writer deliver a powerful thought or piece of information. One principle should govern the use of punctuation: Punctuation when necessary but only when necessary.

The major punctuation marks are the apostrophe, colon, comma, exclamation point, hyphen, parentheses, period, question mark, quotation mark (single and double), and semicolon. Each has a particular set of uses that the good writer should know.

Judge Roberts, sarcastic grammarian

When he was nominated to be Chief Justice of the U.S. Supreme Court in 2005, many thought John Roberts to be a right-wing ideologue with a hidden agenda to roll back many of the liberal-leaning decisions the U.S. Supreme court has made during the last 50 years.

On the other hand, some thought he might be a moderate with great respect for the law, the Constitution and precedent.

Practically no one has yet accused him of being a liberal in conservative's clothing, but with Supreme Court nominees, you never know. After some years on the Court, we still don't know.

John Roberts (White House photo)

But whatever he is, John Roberts is a grammarian.

And that should give us other grammarians -- no matter what our political leanings -- some comfort.

The New York Times, in an article by Anne Kornblut published earlier at the time of his nomination (In Re Grammar, Roberts's Stance is Crystal Clear), reported that an examination of many of the briefs and memos that Roberts has written over the years shows he is extremely precise in his use of the language -- and that he demands such precision of others.

Roberts does not hesitate to correct or critique the language used by his colleagues.

> *A cheerfully ruthless copy editor over the years, Judge Roberts has demanded verbal rigor from his colleagues and subordinates, refusing to tolerate the slightest grammatical slip, and boasting an exceptional vocabulary and command of literature himself.*

The article quotes a former law firm colleague as saying that very little got by Roberts' editing pencil, even Neil Armstrong's famous line when first setting foot on the moon in 1969. Another colleague had quoted it (as it is commonly quoted): "One small step for man, one giant leap for mankind." Roberts remembered it differently and told him so. "It is my recollection that he actually said 'one small step for a man, one giant leap for mankind,' but the 'a' was somewhat garbled in transmission. Without the 'a,' the phrase makes no sense."

And as a good grammarian, Roberts can detect flaws that go beyond the writing.

In a memorandum the next year, responding to a letter from David T. Willard, an elementary school superintendent in Illinois who opposed the administration's education policies, Mr. Roberts again concluded that no legal issues needed to be addressed by the White House counsel. But he took the opportunity to note, "The letter is very sarcastic, although Willard inadvertently proves our point about the quality of public education by incorrectly using 'affect' for 'effect.' "

Roberts himself was being a bit sarcastic, but what's the fun of being a good grammarian for if you can't use a little sarcasm occasionally?

Apostrophe

This mark is most often used to show possession, as in John's book, Sally's cooking, the horse's saddle. When a noun is pluralized with an s, the apostrophe should be placed after the s: the clocks' chiming, the birds' flight.

Do not use an apostrophe to form a plural, as in this incorrect example: The aye's have it.

Colon

The colon is most often used to introduce something. (It has been used a number of times in this capacity in this chapter.) Most often, the colon is used to introduce a list, as in: The flag has three colors: red, white and blue.

Colons are also used to denote time: He will arrive at 11:15 p.m.

Comma

The comma has many uses in English, and it is the punctuation mark that is most likely to give inexperienced writers problems. We have listed some of those uses in the sidebar article for this chapter. While there are specific rules about commas that all writers must learn and apply, in general commas indicate a pause in a thought or the separation of items or ideas. One good way of learning how to use commas is to note how they are used by professional writers.

ESSAY: Rules for using commas

The comma is one of the most important tools of punctuation. If it is used correctly, it can clarify an otherwise confusing piece of writing. The following are some of the common rules and guidelines for using a comma.

Commas separate two independent clauses when used with a coordinate conjunction.
• *The clock struck twelve, and I knew I was in trouble.*
• *No one could predict where he was going with that question, and no one wanted to answer it.*

Commas separate words or items in a list.
• *Mary stuffed the donuts, candy and brownies in her purse.*
• *He decided to take geography, geology and physics all in the same semester.*
Note: No comma before the terminal "and," unless an integral element of the series requires a conjunction.
• *I had orange juice, toast, and ham and eggs for lunch.*

Commas separate coordinate adjectives. They modify the same noun and could sensibly be separated by "and."
• *She described the intruder as a dark, beautiful woman.*

Commas separate words or figures that might be misunderstood. (Be careful about this use.)
• *What the problem is, is not clear.*

Commas set off introductory material.

Prepositional phrase
• *After all of the hardship, he was still unwilling to leave his home.*
Participial phrase
• *Having suffered heavy losses, the enemy withdrew.*
Infinitive phrase
• *To win games, the team decided to double its practice schedule.*
Dependent clause
• *If another strike takes place, the company has threatened to shut down the plant.*

Commas set off words or phrases used as appositives. (An appositive is a word or phrase placed next to another word or phrase as an explanation.)
• *John Smythe, the sole surviving son, now stands to inherit everything.*
• *Gary Hart, the former candidate, will speak at the meeting.*

Commas set off non-essential (non-restrictive) clauses.
• *Mary Jones, the woman standing on the corner, is my cousin.*
• *The latest entrant in the race is James West, who has served two terms in the office and one term in prison.*

Commas set off parenthetical words or phrases.
• *Connective adverbs: However, he found the load too heavy.*
• *Prepositional phrases: He, on the other hand, is a gentleman and a scalawag.*

Commas set off the year in a complete date.
• *The young man was born on Nov. 15, 2001, in Nashville.*

Commas set off a state or country when a city or town name is used.
• *She came here from Dublin, Ireland, when her father bought a toupee factory.*
• *His family moved to Tulsa, Okla., after his arrest for shoplifting a garden hose.*
Note: Commas on both sides of the noun.

Commas set off nominatives of direct address.
• *She said, "You know, Joe, your marsupial is loose."*
• *Susan, where did you hide my potato peeler?*

Commas set off direct questions from attribution or other explanatory matter.
• *"I can't give you a statement until I finish this sandwich," the judge said.*

Commas set off age and address when used in identification format after names.
• *Sam James, 32, 456 First St., was arrested at 2 a.m.*

Do not use a comma when the clause is essential (restrictive).
• *The man who is standing on the corner is my cousin.*
• *The car that is stalled in the parking lot belongs to the nun.*

Do not use a comma with a partial quotation (not an independent clause).
• *He declared that the pie was "better than kissing."*
• *He said that "anyone involved in the crime" would be charged.*

Do not use a comma before a coordinate conjunction in a series.
• *The flag is red, white and blue.*

Do not use a comma between adjectives that are not coordinate. (The adjectives could not be separated by "and" and make sense.)
• *That is a beautiful race horse.*
• *The knife has a sharp cutting edge.*

Exclamation point

The exclamation point is used to end a sentence or expression of strong emotion. It is used most effectively when used very little. Strong emotion is more effectively indicated by the words the writer uses rather than by the punctuation.

Hyphen

The hyphen is a joiner – like a nail but a visible one. Still, many people misuse the hyphen. The most common use is with compound modifiers: newly-minted coin. Note the modifiers in this example come before the noun. If they were to come after the noun, the hyphen would not be necessary. The coin is newly minted.

Sometimes the hyphen is used when a word has a prefix or suffix: anti-intellectual. Knowing when to hyphenate and when not to is often a matter for a writer's stylebook, which we will discuss in the next chapter.

Parentheses

A set of parentheses closes off words that the writer deems less important in the sentence but is still compelled to include it. Parentheses present a peculiar temptation for the writer who believes that the reader should follow his or her fractured thinking. Writers should remember that words in parentheses are a challenge for the reader, and they should use parentheses sparingly. It is better for a writer to think through what he or she has to say, separate those thoughts into discrete units, and present those units to the reader than to burden the reader with a lot of parenthetical expressions.

Period

Writers use periods in a variety of ways, most often to end sentences. In Britain and other parts of the English-speaking world, the period is also call a "full stop," a good description.

Question mark

The question mark ends an interrogatory sentence or to separate a series of questions, as in the following: How shall I travel? By boat? By train? By plane? Or what?

Quotation marks

Quotations marks should be used when the exact words of a speaker or writer are being quoted. Another use of quotations marks is to set off or emphasize a word or set of words from the rest of the sentence. This second usage, while legitimate, should be employed discretely by the writer. Like parentheses, this device can be easily overused.

Semicolon

A semicolon indicates greater separation of thought than a comma. Most commonly a semicolon separates when the individual items are long, have multiple parts or themselves use commas. For instance: The members of the committee are John Smith, Nashville, Tenn.; Mary Green, Tuscaloosa, Ala.; Susan Brown, Knoxville, Tenn.; and Bob White, Emory, Va.

A semicolon can also be used in place of a comma and coordinating conjunction to separate the two independent clauses of a compound sentence.

Common punctuation problems

A number of conventions govern the use of most punctuation marks, and we have listed quite a few of them in the previous section. They should be thoroughly learned and applied to any writing that a student does. The conventions of usage should become the habits of the writer – things the writer does not have to think about but does as naturally as constructing a sentence.

Unfortunately, many students do not reach college with these conventions ingrained and habits formed. Rather, they continue to guess, and they often guess wrong. The following are some of the most common punctuation errors.

Comma splice

A compound sentence contains two independent clauses; that is, two clauses are present that could stand alone as sentences. The most common way to handle this type of sentence is to join these two independent clauses with a comma and a coordinating conjunction, words such as for, and, nor, but, or, yet, and so. Another way to handle the construction is to join the two clauses with a semicolon.

If a writer uses only a comma but no coordinating conjunction, that is called a comma splice or run-on sentence, as in the following:

John followed Mary down the steps, she stopped and turned around.

A comma splice is a major error of punctuation. To avoid such an error, writers need to understand what an independent clause is, how a compound sentence is constructed, and what words are considered to be coordinating conjunctions.

Appositive phrases

An appositive phrase is one that renames a noun. It usually comes immediately after the noun but not always. Appositive phrases should be surrounded by commas when the phrases occur in the middle of a sentence, but too often, writers omit the second comma, as in the following:

Absalom, the son of David died in battle.

The phrase "the son of David" is an appositive phrase, and there should be a comma after the word "David."

Direct quotations and attributions

A direct quotation and attribution often constitute a sentence within a sentence, and this constructions causes some confusion among careless writers. They are tempted to write the following:

"The lights were off for thirty minutes." Thomas said.

This makes the construction into two sentences when it should be only one. There should be a comma after "minutes" rather than a period, and the comma should be placed inside the quotation marks, as in the following:

"The lights were off for thirty minutes," Thomas said.

Commas setting off non-restrictive clauses

A previous chapter discussed restrictive and non-restrictive clauses. The point was made that non-restrictive or non-essential clauses should be set off from the rest of the sentence by commas. Too often, inexperienced writers forget or do not understand this guideline and wind up writing things such as the following:

Barbara who is a friend of mine drove all the way to San Francisco.

The phrase "who is a friend of mine" is non-restrictive in this sentence and should be surrounded by commas.

Commas quiz 1

Where should a comma be placed in these sentences?

1. Abraham Lincoln was elected to his second term in 1864 but he did not serve out his full term.

2. Claude Monet, the famous impressionist painter lived around the turn of the century.

3. After seeing him lying there the boy ran for help.

4. Three of the nation's largest circulation newspapers are USA Today the New York Times and the Wall Street Journal.

5. "She should not have been out that late" the father said.

6. Bill Clinton of Hope, Ark. was elected president in 1992.

7. "Yes I was there when it happened," the witness said defiantly.

8. She cautioned him to be silent not to speak and not even to breathe.

9. He was born in London, England in 1939 and moved to America two years later.

10. The letter said he would arrive on Nov. 15 1980, but he never was seen again.

11. The girl stared at him with a sad longing look in her eyes.

12. The board of trustees decided to raise tuition by $1000 for all students.

13. The lawyer knew her client was innocent but she had no way of proving it.

14. Elated and excited Sara could not believe what she had just heard.

15. "Wow look at that guy run," the man said to his friends.

16. The letter, which arrived yesterday contained some important tax information.

17. The goon hit him hard, really hard on the side of the face.

18. John hurry up; it's nearly time for the train to arrive.

19. John Kennedy 43 was elected president of the United States on Nov. 6, 1960.

20. After hearing the verdict of the jury, the defendant shouted "No, no, no!"

Commas quiz 2

Where should a comma be placed in these sentences?

1. He sat in his easy chair read the paper and slowly went to sleep.

2. I couldn't get over the way he had changed could you?

3. Even though he liked science he did not like to study.

4. Patricia did not however find the joke very funny.

5. Alvin York, the famous hero of World War I was from a small town in Tennessee.

6. Mark Twain's Hannibal, Mo. home attracts thousands of visitors every year.

7. No he could not have seen the crime; he is blind.

8. Well doesn't he look good in his brand new Sunday clothes.

9. The ring which he bought in New York, was loaded with diamonds.

10 Jupiter, the largest planet in the solar system is a cold and desolate place.

11. The dark lonely street created in him a sense of foreboding.

12. His winning the lottery guaratees him $1000 a month for the rest of his life.

13. Walking into the dark house he had no idea where the doors and walls were.

14. Hold it guys; I don't think we should go any further into the cave.

15. The crowd waited nervously around the body and the police finally arrived.

16 The guard did know in fact who the thieves were.

17. His face, which had appeared on many magazine covers was known to practically everyone.

18. The boy from St. Paul, Minn. took the country by storm with his musical ability.

19. Dec. 7 1941 is commemorated each year as the day the Japanese bombed Pearl Harbor.

20. Seeing his ladyship lying on the floor, the butler said "No, this can't be happening."

Punctuation quiz 1

Read the sentence below and decide where a comma should be located. Select the word after which the comma should be placed.
He asked for three things for Christmas a boat, a truck and a game.
things
Christmas
truck

He asked for three things for Christmas: a boat, a truck and a game.
A colon should be placed after "Christmas." It serves to separate the list (boat, truck and game) from the rest of the sentence.

Read the sentence below and decide where a comma should be located. Select the word after which the comma should be placed.

"The congress has acted irresponsibly" the president said.
irresponsibly (between the word and the quotation mark)
irresponsibly (after the quotation mark)
president

The congress has acted irresponsibly," the president said.
A comma should separate a direct quotation from its attribution and should go inside the quotation marks.

Read the sentence below and decide where a semicolon should be located. Select the word after which the semicolon should be placed.
The guest list included George Rye, chairman of the board, Sam Hayes, president, and Max Scott, the company attorney.
included
board, president
Scott
The guest list included George Rye, chairman of the board; Sam Hayes, president; and Max Scott, the company attorney.
A semicolon should be used to separate items in a series that may themselves contain commas.

Read the sentence below and decide where a comma should be located. Select the word after which the comma should be placed.
Y.A. Tittle, one of the great quarterbacks in the history of the National Football League was on hand for the ceremony.
quarterbacks
history
League
Y.A. Tittle, one of the great quarterbacks in the history of the National Football League, was on hand for the ceremony.
A comma should separate an appositive phrase from the rest of the sentence. An appositive phrase is a phrase that renames a noun. In this sentence, the appositive phrase is "one of the great quarterbacks in the history of the National Football League."

Read the sentence below and decide where a comma should be located. Select the word after which the comma should be placed.
Despite the enormous amount of money many of them make the baseball players are threatening to go on strike again this year.
amount

money

make

Despite the enormous amount of money many of them make, the baseball players are threatening to go on strike again this year.

A comma should separate an introductory phrase from the rest of the sentence. Remember, too, that these phrases usually refer to the subject of the sentence.

Read the sentence below and decide where a comma should be located. Select the word after which the comma should be placed.

He sat in his easy chair read the paper and slowly went to sleep.

easy

chair

paper

He sat in his easy chair, read the paper and slowly went to sleep.

Commas should separate items in a series. AP style says that a comma is unnecessary between the next-to-the-last item and the conjunction _ in this case, "paper" and "and."

Read the sentence below and decide where a semicolon should be located. Select the word after which the semicolon should be placed.

The artist could not finish his painting, his hand was hurt.

artist

painting (in addition to the comma)

painting

(instead of the comma)

The artist could not finish his painting; his hand was hurt.

Semicolons may be used to separate two independent clauses when there is no coordinating conjunction. In most cases, a comma is not sufficient for this purpose.

Read the sentence below and decide where a colon should be located. Select the word after which the colon should be placed.

She picked up several items from the store, fish sticks, hamburger, green beans and celery.

items

store (instead of the comma)

store, sticks, hamburger, beans

She picked up several items from the store: fish sticks, hamburger, green beans and celery.

Colons are used to direct attention a series of items and to separate that series from the rest of the sentence. This can avoid confusing the reader.

Read the sentence below and decide where a semicolon should be located. Select the word after which the semicolon should be placed.

If he doesn't come back soon, we won't be going, if we have to, we'll make other plans.

soon (instead of the comma)

going (instead of the comma)

to (instead of the comma)

If he doesn't come back soon, we won't be going; if we have to, we'll make other plans.

In this sentence each of the independent clauses comes after a dependent clause. The semicolon is use to separate the first independent clause from the second dependent clause.

Punctuation quiz 2

Read the sentence below and decide where a semicolon should be located. Select the word after which the semicolon should be placed.

Nothing hurts worse than rejection, however, we can usually recover from it.

rejection (instead of the comma)

however (instead of the comma)

recover

Nothing hurts worse than rejection; however, we can usually recover from it.

Words and phrases such as "however," "on the contrary" and "on the other hand" are not coordinating conjunctions and are not sufficient for separating two independent clauses. A semicolon is necessary.

Read the sentence below and decide where a colon should be located. Select the word after which the colon should be placed.

The constitution guarantees many rights, a quick and public trial, freedom of speech and the press, the right to petition the government and the right of states to legislate.

rights (instead of the comma)

press

government

The constitution guarantees many rights: a quick and public trial, freedom of speech and the press, the right to petition the government and the right of states to legislate.

The colon in this sentence is used to introduce a series of items. It lets the reader know where that series begins.

Read the sentence below and decide where a semicolon should be located. Select the word after which the semicolon should be placed.

She had a sad and bored look, therefore, none of the men asked her to dance.

sad

look (instead of the comma)

men

She had a sad and bored look; therefore, none of the men asked her to dance.

Here is another case where an interjectory word, "therefore" is not a coordinating conjunction. It alone cannot separate two independent clauses. A semicolon is necessary.

Read the sentence below and decide where a semicolon should be located. Select the word after which the semicolon should be placed.

The lawyer questioned witnesses, she produced evidence for her client, she made an impassioned argument, still, her client was found guilty.
witnesses
witnesses, client, argument (instead of the commas)
still (instead of the comma)
The lawyer questioned witnesses; she produced evidence for her client; she made an impassioned argument; still, her client was found guilty.
If there were a coordinating conjunction such as "and" or "but" in place of "still," the sentence would be correct. Because "still" is not a coordinating conjunction, the series needs to be separated with semicolons.

Read the sentence below and decide where a comma should be located. Select the word after which the comma should be placed.
The disk was stuck in the machine and the DVD was ruined.
stuck
machine
and
The disk was stuck in the machine, and the DVD was ruined.
A comma should be placed before a coordinating conjunction that separates joins to independent clauses.

Read the sentence below and decide where a period should be located. Select the word after which the period should be placed.
The Supreme Court's decision in the case of Baker vs Carr changed the nature of state legislatures.
Supreme
decision
vs
The Supreme Court's decision in the case of Baker vs. Carr changed the nature of state legislatures.
A period is sometimes used after an abbreviation. In this sentence, Baker vs. Carr is a legal case, and the "vs." is short for "versus."

Read the sentence below and decide where a comma should be located. Select the word after which the comma should be placed.
The fire was blamed on the small child who was only three years old.
blamed
small
child
The fire was blamed on the small child, who was only three years old.
A comma or set of commas should separate a non-restrictive clause from the rest of the sentence. A non-restrictive clause is a clause that is not necessary to the meaning of the sentence.

Read the sentence below and decide where a period should be located. Select the word after which the period should be placed.
You must bring a variety of items -- paper, pencils, books, notes, etc -- to the exam.

items
etc
No additional period is necessary.
You must bring a variety of items -- paper, pencils, books, notes, etc. -- to the exam.
The abbreviation "etc." means "and other things" and always takes a period.

Read the sentence below and decide where a period should be located. Select the word after which the period should be placed.
Joseph P Kennedy Jr, the brother of the future president, was killed during World War II.
P"
"P" and "Jr
president
Joseph P. Kennedy Jr., the brother of the future president, was killed during World War II.
The "P" and "Jr" are abbreviations that need periods.

Read the sentence below and decide where a comma should be located. Select the word after which the comma should be placed.
Never have we been showered with more gifts food and cards than this past Christmas.
gifts
both gifts and food
cards
Never have we been showered with more gifts, food and cards than this past Christmas.
A comma should separate the items in a series, but the comma is not necessary between the next-to-last item and the conjunction.

Grammar and punctuation quiz 1

He finally decided that, well it could have been worse.
run-on sentence
sentence fragment
subject-verb agreement
pronoun-antecedent agreement
incorrect or lack of comma(s)
other punctuation problem
misuse of pronoun(s)
incorrect possessive
The "well" in this sentence is an interjection and should be set off from the rest of the sentence by commas.

Andres Segovia, one of the finest guitarists of the 20th century and, too, an expert on Johann S. Bach.
run-on sentence
sentence fragment

71

subject-verb agreement
pronoun-antecedent agreement
incorrect or lack of comma(s)
other punctuation problem
misuse of pronoun(s)
incorrect possessive
This sentence does not have a verb and does not express a complete thought. Therefore, it is a sentence fragment.

The hour is too early, the coffee is too cold.
run-on sentence
sentence fragment
subject-verb agreement
pronoun-antecedent agreement
incorrect or lack of comma(s)
other punctuation problem
misuse of pronoun(s)
incorrect possessive
This sentence has two independent clauses. They should be separated by either a coordinating conjunction and a comma or a semicolon.

The team climbed onto the bus, celebrating their victory with loud singing and shouting.
run-on sentence
sentence fragment
subject-verb agreement
pronoun-antecedent agreement
incorrect or lack of comma(s)
other punctuation problem
misuse of pronoun(s)
incorrect possessive
The antecedent in this sentence is "team," and because it is a singular noun, it should have a singular pronoun. The "their" is incorrect; it should be "its."

I doubt that whomever stole the watch is going to return it.
run-on sentence
sentence fragment
subject-verb agreement
pronoun-antecedent agreement
incorrect or lack of comma(s)
other punctuation problem
misuse of pronoun(s)
incorrect possessive
The pronoun "whomever" in this sentence should be "whoever" because it is the subject of the subordinate clause.

Both the music and the moon was beautiful that night as ships quietly slipped in and

out of the harbor.
run-on sentence
sentence fragment
subject-verb agreement
pronoun-antecedent agreement
incorrect or lack of comma(s)
other punctuation problem
misuse of pronoun(s)
incorrect possessive
This sentence has a compound subject and the coordinating conjunction "and." The verb in this case should be the plural "was" rather than the singular "is."

Dr and Mrs Charles Reynolds were the guests honored by the civic clubs last night.
run-on sentence
sentence fragment
subject-verb agreement
pronoun-antecedent agreement
incorrect or lack of comma(s)
other punctuation problem
misuse of pronoun(s)
incorrect possessive
A period should be placed after the abbreviations "Dr." and "Mrs."

A lawyer can easily handle a problem such as that, but getting an appointment with them is easy.
run-on sentence
sentence fragment
subject-verb agreement
pronoun-antecedent agreement
incorrect or lack of comma(s)
other punctuation problem
misuse of pronoun(s)
incorrect possessive
The subject of this sentence is "lawyer," a singular noun; its antecedent should also be singular. In this case, the "them" should be replaced with "one."

There were too many books on the shelf; too many papers on his desk; too many magazines on the floor; and too much clutter all over the room.
run-on sentence
sentence fragment
subject-verb agreement
pronoun-antecedent agreement
incorrect or lack of comma(s)
other punctuation problem
misuse of pronoun(s)
incorrect possessive
The semicolons are not necessary in this sentence. Even though the items in the

series are long one, they can be separated by commas. Instead of semicolons, commas should be placed after "shelf" and "desk." No punctuation is needed after "floor."

Grammar and punctuation quiz 2

By striking the clock signaled to us that it was time to leave.
run-on sentence
sentence fragment
subject-verb agreement
pronoun-antecedent agreement
incorrect or lack of comma(s)
other punctuation problem
misuse of pronoun(s)
incorrect possessive
A comma should be used to separate an introductory phrase from the rest of the sentence. In this case, the comma should be placed after "striking." Notice how confusing this sentence is when there is no comma.

Joe appreciated him recognizing the achievements of the the club to which he belonged.
run-on sentence
sentence fragment
subject-verb agreement
pronoun-antecedent agreement
incorrect or lack of comma(s)
other punctuation problem
misuse of pronoun(s)
incorrect possessive
As a general rule, a possessive pronoun should be used before a gerund. In this sentence, the pronoun should be "his" rather than "him." The gerund is "recognizing."
Joe appreciated his recognizing the achievements of the club to which he belonged.

The radio station changed their format from top 40 to oldies last year.
run-on sentence
sentence fragment
subject-verb agreement
pronoun-antecedent agreement
incorrect or lack of comma(s)
other punctuation problem
misuse of pronoun(s)
incorrect possessive
The mistake in this sentence is one of the most common made in both written and spoken English. The pronoun "their" should be "its" because the pronoun's antecedent, "station," is singular.

Either the money or the fame are certain to bring him sadness in the end.
run-on sentence
sentence fragment
subject-verb agreement
pronoun-antecedent agreement
incorrect or lack of comma(s)
other punctuation problem
misuse of pronoun(s)
incorrect possessive
A compound subject joined by the construction "either . . . or" usually takes a
singular verb. That's because the subject is one or the other, not both. The verb in
this sentence should be "is."

George C. Scott, a fine actor was an Academy Award for his performance in Patton.
run-on sentence
sentence fragment
subject-verb agreement
pronoun-antecedent agreement
incorrect or lack of comma(s)
other punctuation problem
misuse of pronoun(s)
incorrect possessive
The phrase "a fine actor" is an appositive phrase; that is, it renames the noun
"George C. Scott." Appositive phrases should be set off from the rest of the sentence
by commas. A comma should be placed after the word "actor."

Whom did he say was coming to the reception?
run-on sentence
sentence fragment
subject-verb agreement
pronoun-antecedent agreement
incorrect or lack of comma(s)
other punctuation problem
misuse of pronoun(s)
incorrect possessive
The "whom" in this sentence should be "who" because it is used as the subject of the
clause. You would say "who was coming to the reception," not "whom was coming to
the reception."

He did not find any trace of the body, did he.
run-on sentence
sentence fragment
subject-verb agreement
pronoun-antecedent agreement
incorrect or lack of comma(s)
other punctuation problem
misuse of pronoun(s)

incorrect possessive
The sentence should end with a question mark because of the interrogatory phrase at the end.

The game, we played, is the same one that has been played for many centuries.
run-on sentence
sentence fragment
subject-verb agreement
pronoun-antecedent agreement
incorrect or lack of comma(s)
other punctuation problem
misuse of pronoun(s)
incorrect possessive
The commas in this sentence are unnecessary because the clause "we played" is a restrictive clause.

The executive comes from Nashville, Tenn. but now lives in New York City.
run-on sentence
sentence fragment
subject-verb agreement
pronoun-antecedent agreement
incorrect or lack of comma(s)
other punctuation problem
misuse of pronoun(s)
incorrect possessive
When a city and state are mentioned in the middle of a sentence, a comma should separate the state from the rest of the sentence. The period after "Tenn." is also necessary because it is an abbreviation.
The executive comes from Nashville, Tenn., but now lives in New York City.

ESSAY: An expensive comma

Sometimes punctuation can be expensive.

That was certainly the case for Rogers Communications of Canada, which recently found that its misreading of a contract -- not recognizing the meaning of the placement of a comma in a particular sentence of a contract -- will cost the company a couple of million dollars. All this is according an article in the Toronto Globe and Mail.

Rogers had a contract to put cable lines across thousands of utility polls in the Maritimes. Rogers thought the agreement was good for at least five years because of the sentence that the agreement "shall continue in force for a period of five years from the date it is made, and thereafter for successfive year terms, unless and until terminated by one year prior notice in writing by either party."

The contract was with Aliant, Inc. More than a year before the contract dispute, Aliant informed Rogers that it was giving notice that it was scrapping the contract based on that sentence. Rogers argued that its understanding was that the contract, which was still in its first five-year period, could not be discarded so easily.

But the Canadian Radio-television and Telecommunications Commission disagreed.

The comma, the commission said, gave Aliant the right to cancel the contract during the first five years with only a year's notice. Alient did so, and renotiating the contract cost Rogers about $2 million.

That's a high price to pay for overlooking a comma.

Terms

punctuation	run-on sentence
comma	prepositional phrase
apostrophe	possessive
appositive	direct quotation
semicolon	attribution
comma splice	

Tools of the Writer: Spelling

To spell a word correct is an essential skill of the professional writer. It is one of the chief expectations of the reader. There is no substitute for correct spelling.

Expensive misspellings

Not double-checking your spelling can turn out to be an expensive proposition.

That's what the folks in Livermore, Calif., found out in 2004 when they spent $40,000 for a mosaic for their new library. The artwork contained 175 words, many of them names of writers, scientists and artists. Eleven of those words were misspelled.

They included Shakespeare (Shakespere), Einstein (Eistein), and Gauguin (Gaugan).

The Miami artist who executed the work at first claimed artistic license (maybe some of your students have used the same excuse) but later said she would fix the problem words. Unfortunately, the city of Livermore had to pay her an extra $6,000 plus expenses to do that.

An ongoing struggle

Most of us are still learning to spell.

That's because English is such a dynamic language. Just a few years ago, many of us (who can remember that far) did not know what a web site was, and we certainly weren't worried about how to spell it. Today, we have to decide: is it website or web site (one word or two). The jury is still out. The Associated Press Stylebook says it's two words, but if you put "web site" into a Google search, it will ask you if you don't really mean "website."

Who knows what we will be faced with next year – or even next month. What new word or concept will we have to master?

As with other facets of language use, spelling presents the professional writer with peculiar difficulties. Most of us struggle to some extent, even though some are better than others at remembering the correct spelling of many words. We memorize words, forget them, memorize them again, and then wind up looking them up anyway. We try a variety of devices for getting spelling right, and yet we still misspell words.

Yet spelling is like grammar and punctuation when it comes to our audience. They will assume that we, the writers, are perfect and tend to ignore it when we are. When we are less than perfect, the audience will judge us to be idiots.

It's not as if there aren't rules. There are plenty of rules. The problem is that there are plenty of exceptions to each of the rules. And the exceptions are not minor. They occur with words that we use every day. Here are some of the rules (and a few exceptions):

- I before E except after C.
- Double the final consonant when adding an ending to a word. (plan, planned)
- Drop the final E when adding a syllable beginning with a vowel. (come, coming)
- Change the final Y to I when adding a syllable to a word. (army, armies; exceptions, shy, shyness, play, played)
- Retain a double consonant when adding a symbol to a word. (full, fullness; ebb, ebbing)
- The plural for most words is formed by adding S.
- Words that end with S, Z, X, CH, or SH usually get their plurals by adding ES.
- Never use an apostrophe and S to form a plural for a word that is fully spelled out.

There are many more statements we could make about how words are spelled. Such statements in reality are not rules. They are better described as "general happenings." They are the way we do things most of the time, but they do not mean that new words will always conform.

The spelling of words today is an indicator of the history of the language and the anarchic way in which it has developed. English has received contributions from many lands and languages. Words have evolved and changed over time. Sometimes their meaning and pronunciation evolved, but the spelling did not.

All well and good – but what is the professional writer to do? We offer the following as some general principles with regard to spelling:

Select one spelling – the most commonly accepted one – for any word and use that one. The most common one is usually the first entry in a good dictionary.

Pronunciation can sometimes help, but don't count on it. In English, many words are definitely not spelled the way they are pronounced, and pronunciation can vary from place to place. No one spells Boston with an "a," but native of the city often pronounce it that way.

Capitalize as little as possible. Proper names and words that begin sentences should be capitalized, of course. Beyond that, try to keep your pinkies off the shift key.

Use your word processor's spellcheck program – and then use your brain. Any piece of writing worth reading by an audience is worth reading a second or third time by the writer. Edit, edit, edit. We'll have more to say about this later.

Beyond all that, continue learning to spell. It's a lifelong mission.

A matter of credibility

Knowing and applying the rules of English, including spelling rules, is not just a matter of intellectual pride or rigor – although it is certainly that. We should strive for perfection in the use of the language because our psyches will allow us to accept nothing less.

But the correct use of the language enhances our credibility with our audiences and is a major factor in establishing our authority to speak to them. That credibility and authority can become a most valuable asset, particularly in a profession and discipline for which education – and appearing to be educated – is among the highest of values.

Questions for discussion

1. What image of grammar and grammarians did you form in grade school or high school?

2. The author makes a strong case for knowing the rules of grammar, but some people do not think this knowledge is very important. The author believes that you can write well without knowing these rules. What do you think?

3. The text says there are some times when a sentence fragment might be appropriate. When would that be?

4. What do you think are the most important rules for using a comma?

5. Explain the difference between its, it's, and its'.

6. Make a list of words that you think should be spelled differently.

7. Make a list of words that you often hear people misusing. Why do you think people misuse them?

8. What is the rule of grammar, spelling or punctuation that you would most like to abolish?

Spelling quiz 1

Select the word that is spelled correctly.
releive
releve
* relieve
Use i before e except after c or when sounded like ay, as in neighbor and weigh.

* desiring
desireing
desirieng
The original form, spelled desire, falls under the rule for adding suffixes which applies generally as follows: drop a final silent e when adding a suffix that begins

with a vowel.

achievment
* achievement
achieviment
The original form of the word is spelled achieve. When adding suffixes, keep the final e if the suffix begins with a consonant.

* comedies
comedys
comedyes
When adding -s to words ending in y, you generally change the y to i when the y is preceded by a consonant.

changeble
* changeable
changable
Their are a few words which are exceptions to the adding of the e suffix rule. Examples of such words are changeable, judgment, argument, and truly.

plaied
playyed
* played
When adding -ed to words ending in y, ordinarily change y to i when the y is preceded by a consonant but not when it is preceded by a vowel.

occurence
occurrience
* occurrence
If a final consonant is preceded by a single vowel and the consonant ends a one-syllable word or a stressed syllable, double the consonant when adding a suffix beginning with a vowel.

Spiveyes
Spiveies
* Spiveys
With proper names ending in y, do not change the y to i even if it is preceded by a consonant.
* churches
churchs
churchies
Add -s to form the plurals of most nouns; add -es to singular nouns ending in -s, -ch, -sh, -x.

heros
* heroes
heroies

Ordinarily add -s to nouns ending in -o when the o is preceded by a vowel. Add -es when it is preceded by a consonant.

* mothers-in-law
mother-in-laws
mothers-in-laws
To form the plural of a hyphenated compound word, add the -s to the chief word even if it does not appear at the end.

* criteria
criterion
criterions
Some words in the English language retain their written plural forms as they were in the language from which they were derived.

foriegn
* foreign
foregn
The word foreign is an exception to the i before e rule. Some other examples of exceptions are seize, either, weird, height, and leisure.

realy
* really
realiy
Do not drop a final -l when you add -ly.

thiefs
* thieves
thiefes
To form the plural of some nouns ending in f or fe, change the ending to ve before adding the -s.

noticable
noticiable
* noticeable
To keep the sound of -ce or of -ge, do not drop the final e before -able or -ous.

acrege
acrage
* acreage
The word acreage is an exception to the general e suffix rules. Other exceptions include mileage, argument, ninth, truly and wholly.

studing
studeing
* studying
Do not change -y to -i before adding the suffix -ing.

beneffited
benefitted
* benefited
When multiple syllable words are not stressed on the last syllable but the consonant is preceded by a single vowel, you will not double the last consonant.

echos
* echoes
echoies
While most nouns ending in -o just require the addition of -s to make them plural there are a few exceptions. Examples are echoes, heroes, vetoes and potatoes.

Terms

Associated Press Stylebook

dictionary

credibility

audience

vowel

consonant

capital

lowercase

spellcheck

pronunciation

plural

Writing Like a Journalist

This book is about writing — first and foremost, how to write well in a professional environment. Secondly, it's about how learning how to write in the major forms of writing demanded by the mass media.

The Four Horsemen of Notre Dame

Outlined against a blue-gray October sky, the Four Horsemen rode again. In dramatic lore they are known as Famine, Pestilence, Destruction, and Death. These are only aliases. Their real names are Stuhldreher, Miller, Crowley and Layden.

That's how Grantland Rice, sports writer for the New York Tribune, began his account of the Notre Dame-Army football game of 1924. Notre Dame, led by its great backfield, won the game against a strong team from the United States Military Academy (Army).

Rice was fond of using literary allusions in his writing, and this one comes from the Book of Revelation in the Bible.

Four Horsemen of Notre Dame

No paragraph in the history of sports journalism has been quoted more than this one. The "Four Horsemen" became part of the legend of Notre Dame football, and publicists at the University placed the four footballers on four horses for a famous photograph. And that photograph was turned into a postage stamp more than 50 years later.

Rice was just one of a number of great sports writers who have graced the pages of American newspaper. Ring Lardner and Damon Runyon, whose fiction is now studied in literature classes, were sports writers of the top rank.

Besides Rice, two others who were especially notable were Red Smith and Shirley Povich.

Smith, who ended his career with the New York Times, was hired by the New York Herald Tribune in 1945 and covered sports and sports figures with intelligence and sensitivity. His column became the most widely syndicated of the age.

Smith cared about his writing. On purpose, he wrote simply and elegantly. And he knew how hard it is to do that. He once said there is nothing to writing -- all you have to do is sit down at a typewriter and "open a vein."

Povich covered sports for the Washington Post for most of the last century and knew every major sports figure from Babe Ruth to Michael Jordon. He, too, wrote sensitively, elegantly and simply. And he wasn't afraid to express his opinions about what he saw.

In 1960, disgusted that his hometown Washington Redskins were the last National Football League team to integrate, Povich wrote the following about the Skins game with the Cleveland Browns.:

For 18 minutes the Redskins were enjoying equal rights with the Cleveland Browns yesterday, in the sense that there was no score in the contest. Then it suddenly became unequal in favor of the Browns, who brought along Jim Brown, their rugged colored fullback from Syracuse.

From 25 yards out, Brown was served the ball by Milt Plum on a pitch-out and he integrated the Redskins' goal line with more than deliberate speed, perhaps exceeding the famous Supreme Court decree. Brown fled the 25 yards like a man in an uncommon hurry and the Redskins' goal line, at least, became interracial.

Why journalistic writing is different

Why is writing so important to journalism?

• Journalism begins with reporting.
• Reporting is a skill that reaches beyond journalism.
• Writing is central to all media industries.
• Writing is the mark of a well educated person.
• Writing is a powerful activity. The ability to control and articulate ideas

and information gives you power over what other people know and think about.

What's different?

Writing journalistically is different from all other writing you have had in four important ways:

First, it emphasizes information. The major purpose of writing for the mass media is to present information.

This information should be
– recent
– verifiable
– medium specific

Second, journalistic writing is done in a professional environment. One of the purposes of this book is to teach you how to report and write professionally. That is, we want you to understand what the demands of professionalism are and what you will need to meet those demands.

Third, writing in a media environment usually means writing for a mass audience. Chances are, a lot of people are going to read or hear or see what you write (not just an English professor). Understanding that audience is a big part of learning to write for the mass media.

Finally, there is the concept of **modesty**. (Check out Invisible Writing in Chapter 1.) By that we mean that good writing for the mass media puts the writer in the background and emphasizes instead the content of the writing. An audience doesn't care what you think or how you feel about what you are writing. The audience wants information, and it wants that information presented accurately, completely, efficiently and precisely.

Writing that is modest
– doesn't call attention to itself
– doesn't call attention to the writer or to the form
– emphasizes the content and not the writer's style
– is generally free of the opinion of the writer

Four characteristics of media writing

- accuracy
- clarity
- efficiency
- precision

We've already covered these concepts in an earlier section of this book, but we need to review and re-emphasize them here.

Accuracy is the chief requirement of a writer for the mass media. This is not just a journalist's requirement. All writers are expected to present information accurately and to take some pains in doing so. Many of the procedures for writing for the mass media are set up to ensure accuracy.

Clarity means that you should present your information using commonly understood words and phrases and in a context so that it can be easily understood by a mass audience. Your writing should answer all of the questions that could be expected by the audience. (Not all of the questions that could be asked, but all those that it takes to understand the information.)

Efficiency is one of the most prized writing characteristics. Efficiency means using the fewest words to present information accurately and clearly. Efficiency is difficult to achieve because

* most of us write inefficiently, especially on first draft
* most of use do not do a good job in editing our writing
* the world is filled with inefficient writing, and we often fall victim to it.

Precision means that as a writer, you take special care with the language. You know good grammar and practice it. You use words for precisely what they mean. You develop a love for the language.

How do we learn to exhibit these characteristics in our writing?

First, we pay attention to the basics.

The world in which we report

The major fact about journalism these days is the development of digital news media. The environment in which journalism is practiced and produced is changing radically from what it was five or 10 years ago. This change may not be as apparent to you as it is to those who are 30 years old and older, but it is palpable and important.

So how do we understand this change?

One way is by comparing the web (and its mobile descendants) to what is now termed the traditional media (newspapers, magazines, radio and television, etc.). Here are some of the characteristics of the web as a news medium that we must understand:

- **Capacity.** The web can handle more material than either print or broadcast.

- **Flexibility.** The web is a platform for a variety of forms – text, audio, photos, audio and video – and journalists must decide what form to use to present their information.

- **Immediacy.** The web is an immediate medium; information can be posted immediately, even as events are in progress, and journalists must learn how to do this.

- **Permanence.** Nothing on the web need be lost, and everything that is on the web is retrievable and easily duplicated.

- **Interactivity.** Readers, users and other journalists can contribute to the coverage of a topic or event;

- **Linkage.** Journalists tap the power of the web when they learn how to link their content to other information.

- **Mobility.** Cellphones and hand-held devices are the medium of choice for many news consumers; journalists who want to communicate with them have to understand the nature of this mobility.

The world of journalism is changing as we speak. No one has a good handle of what it will be like a year or three years from now.

ESSAY: A good take on being a journalist

A good take on being a journalist

Reporting is where journalism begins.

Without reporting -- gather facts, information, and views and putting all those together -- journalism doesn't exist. So we owe a deep debt to those who spend their lives doing the tough job of reporting.

Deborah Howell, former ombudsman for the Washington Post, has a good take on what it takes to be a reporter in one of her columns.

What makes a good reporter? Endless curiosity and a deep need to know what is happening. Then, the ability to hear a small clue and follow it. When Post reporter Dana Priest first heard "a tiny, tiny piece" of what turned out to be the Walter Reed Army Medical Center scandal, she couldn't ignore it.

She also quotes former Post editor Ben Bradlee, not a bad reporter himself:

They've got to love what they're doing; they've got to be serious about turning over rocks, opening doors. The story drives you. It's part of your soul.

Read the whole thing.

Basic principles of journalistic writing

People who work in news

- do highly important work;

- are sometimes not very popular;

- have a real and sometimes immediate impact on people and society at large;

- provide society with accurate information and serve as independent observers;

- work very, very hard.

Writing in the media environment

Professional writers need to learn what it is to write in the media environment. This "environment" is not just a place — although it is often that, such as a television or newspaper newsroom or the writer's pool of an advertising agency. But it is also a state of mind, an acculturation that the writer must undergo.

In this section we'll discuss what it means to become acculturated as a media writer.

Purpose of media writing

The purpose of media writing is not self expression, although sometimes that is involved in your writing. The chief purpose of media writing is **to inform the reader.** It is to present information and ideas.

Two secondary purposes are **persuasion** and **entertainment**, but what lies behind almost all media writing is information.

How do we present information? That's what we're going to learn more about in this section of the course. Here are some of the key concepts we will cover:

* Information, the chief purpose of the writer.
* Accuracy, the chief goal of writer.
* The writer as a "third person" or impersonal presence in the writing.
* Writing for an audience, always.
* Conventions and practices of media writing.
* Steps in the writing process.
* Unity and transitions.

The media writer's job is to gather, process and present information.

The first and foremost consideration in the processing and presenting of information is accuracy. Getting information right means understanding that information in its appropriate context. Many of the practices, customs and conventions of media writing are designed to ensure accuracy and to convince the reader that information is accurate.

Conventions and practices

Part of becoming a media writer is to learn the conventions practiced by most writers for the mass media. You also need to learn some of the concepts and principles that underlie these practices.

• **Objectivity and fairness.**Part of presenting information is doing so without injecting your own beliefs or feelings into the writing. Media writers try to present information in a manner that does not reveal how they feel about it or what they think. Their job is to let readers or viewers make up their minds about what the information may mean. They go into what might be called a third person mode — writing impersonally, de-emphasizing the writer and emphasizing the information.

That's why one of the major writing conventions is to let readers know where information is coming from. Sources of information and attribution are important parts of the media writing mix. In the weeks ahead, you will learn how to attribute information to a source when you are writing news and information. This is one of the most common practices of a media.

• **Editing.** Writing is an individual act, but in the media environment, it does not remain with the individual. Most media organizations have some kind of editing process. Other people will get involved with your writing. They will edit and question it. They may rewrite it. This is part of the process, and writers need to get used to it.

Editing begins with the individual writer, however. Few people can write in a way that does not need editor. The good writer learns to recognize the weaknesses of the first draft and to take care in correcting them. As a student of journalistic writing, you should get into the good habit of editing your work carefully. Learn to recognize the technical mistakes you might make, but also read you copy for wordiness, logic and coherence.

When you edit your work: Instead of telling yourself, "I'm going to find the mistakes," tell yourself, "I'm going to make this better."

• **Time, space and deadlines.** Almost all media writing is done under fairly strict deadline pressure. Newspaper reporters must meet daily deadlines. Broadcast reporters must meet hourly deadlines. Advertising copy writers and public relations practitioners must always meet media deadlines.

But, you might argue, if I just had a little more time, I could do a better job. That argument is heard throughout the professional world. And, it might be true.

The problem, of course, is that if we didn't have deadlines, few newspapers, magazines, newscasts, advertisements or newsletters would get produced. Deadlines make the process of producing these things more efficient and predictable. The mass media couldn't work without deadlines.

So, get used to them.

Start developing habits that let you function more efficiently. Read with great concentration; learn to block out distractions. Get into the habit of developing your writing sentence by sentence, rather than word by word. Later in the course, we will talk about how to edit more efficiently.

• **Writing for an audience.** It may seem obvious, but the media writer must keep in mind that the writing is done for an audience — usually a mass audience. The writing will be read or heard by many people.

That imposes a great restraint on the writer, who must always ask, "What does the audience want? What does it expect? What must I do to satisfy the audience?"

Again, the point is that media writing is not done for self-fulfillment. It is done for a purpose of serving a large audience in some way.

Characteristics of a media writer

Successful media writing reveals the following characteristics about the writer:

- maturity — an understanding of the responsibilities of the writer who asks that the audience invest its time and its money in what he or she is doing
- knowledge of the language
- knowledge of all forms of media writing and understanding of the proper use of these forms
- willingness to risk having his or her efforts subjected to the judgment of a large audience

Writing coherently

Clear, coherent writing takes practice and effort. Most of us can speak well enough to be understood by our friends and acquaintances. Writing is a different matter. To say what we want to say in writing involves an enormous intellectual effort.

One of the things that helps media writers is that they use particular forms acceptable to certain media. For instance, the first form we will be learning in JEM200 is the "inverted pyramid."

Along with knowledge of the form, we must understand what we are writing about. That is, we should have a thorough knowledge of the facts, information and ideas that we are trying to present with our writing. Often, we will be asked to string a set of facts together in a unified way, and the technical tool we use for this is the transition.

There are several major forms of transitions. It is not important that you know them by name, but it is important that you understand how they work and when they should be used. They are

* connectors
* hooks
* pronouns
* associations
* logic

Three steps for improving your writing

As we begin the section on newswriting, you should do three things:

- **Read** examples of good newswriting; your texts provide you with many examples of inverted pyramid news stories; and there is also the newspaper and the Internet.
- **Analyze** these articles in light of what we have been telling you; look for examples of clear writing, good lead paragraphs, use of transitions, efficient writing, etc.
- **Emulate**; copy. Try to do the same things in your writing that you have seen in the writing of others. Make your stories like the examples in the book.

ESSAY: The writing life, Gay Talese style

For more than 40 years, there has been intense interest in the writing style exemplified by Gay Talese – and in Gay Talese (web site) himself.

But that emphasis, particularly in Talese himself, may have been misplaced. Talese is certainly a writer of utmost grace. He works at his profession with an intensity that is rare.-

But what distinguishes him is not his writing but his reporting.

Talese has produced a number of important and interesting magazine articles and books, most famously "Frank Sinatra has a cold" (Esquire, April 1966), *The Kingdom and the Power, Honor Thy Father,* and *Thy Neighbor's Wife,* among many others. In some of these, he has been a minor or major character.

Now he has published a memoir, **A Writer's Life,** which talks about his methods of reporting and writing. When it was published, the book and Talese were profiled in the New York Times ("Gay

... In the late 60's, when he was working on "Honor Thy Father," his book about the Bonanno crime family, he moved in for a while with Bill Bonanno and his bodyguards, and in the early 80's, while working on "Unto the Sons," he suddenly decamped for Calabria. Most famously, in the early 70's, while working on "Thy Neighbor's Wife," a book about sexual liberation in America, he went native for an extended period — far longer, his critics claimed, than his research strictly required — managing massage parlors in New York and living for a while at Sandstone, a nudist swingers' colony in California.

Talese is a graduate of the University of Alabama, where I taught for 25 years. Several years ago, he returned to campus to receive a writing award that my college gave him, and two of my faculty colleagues and I had dinner with him one evening.

I told him the story of when I was an undergraduate at the University of Tennessee in 1970 and had just finished The Kingdom and the Power. The book had been written like a novel, and I wondered how he could have gotten inside the minds of all of the people he described in the book. He had to have speculated or made good guesses, I thought.

No, he said, there was nothing in the book that he had made up or speculated on; everything was the result of interviews (sometimes many interviews) and observation.

Talese went on in that conversation to describe his work methods, which include intensive concentration on his subjects and hours of taking and transcribing notes. He is meticulous in the construction of his sentences and paragraphs, revising and constantly questioning his prose. His standards are high, exacting and tortuous.

But Talese doesn't make it up. He is not a novelist, although as a pioneer of the New Journalism writing style, he uses some of the techniques of fiction. He is a journalist, and as he said recently, "Nonfiction takes no liberty with the facts."

Above all, Talese is a reporter.

The inverted pyramid

Understanding the forms in which news and information should be placed in journalistic writing and handling those forms with confidence is the mark of a media writer. In a previous section, we suggested that the way to learn to write for the mass media is to do three things:

- **Read**
- **Analyze**
- **Emulate**

It's good to remind ourselves of that approach as we get into reporting because reporting and writing go hand-in-hand.

So what about the inverted pyramid?

The inverted pyramid is an anti-narrative structure of writing about events. Instead of starting at the beginning, the inverted pyramid structure demands that you begin with the most important information and that you present information in decreasing order of importance.

Some historians argue that the inverted pyramid form developed in the mid-19th century when news was first being transmitted by telegraph wires. The wires were unreliable — or during the Civil War would be taken over by the military — so a style of presentation had to be used that would get the most important information out first. The outcome of a battle might be the most important thing that happened during the battle. But

Inverted pyramid

Most important information

Next most important information

Less important information

Inverted pyramid news stories require that the most important information be put in the lead paragraph.

rather than writing a narrative that delayed telling what happened until the very end, the journalist had to say it at the beginning of the report.

Today the inverted pyramid structure is highly developed and widely used, not just in newspapers and wire services but in many kinds of writing. Many business letters, for instance, use an inverted pyramid structure.

Lead paragraph

The most important part of an inverted pyramid news story is the lead paragraph. Most lead paragraphs should be one sentence and a maximum of 30 to 35 words. Those are the technical requirements. The content requirement is that it tell the most important piece of information that occurred in the event.

In addition, a lead should contain the main who, what, when and where of the story. And leads should

- be direct and simple; they should have the most important information near the beginning of the sentence;
- not try to tell everything, but they should be good summaries of what the story is about;
- include specific information — concrete facts — about the story;
- not begin with the when element because this is rarely the most important thing you have to tell the reader;
- use a strong verb to describe the action;
- should be accurate — above all else.

The second paragraph

The second paragraph is where you develop some idea or piece of information that is in the lead.

You should not drop into a narrative in the second paragraph. Many students concentrate on writing good leads but then have a tendency to start at the beginning in the second paragraph.

Resist that temptation.

Remember that you are presenting information in decreasing order of importance. Each new paragraph should present the reader with some new information. But it should be tied to the previous paragraph by the skillful use of transitions.

Inverted pyramid checklist

As you learn to write in the inverted pyramid structure, you should take a look at the inverted pyramid checklist. These are some of the most common mistakes that beginning students make in writing their news stories. This is a good list to have beside you when you finish a story, and you should not turn it in until you have gone over this list. Information should be presented in descending order of importance.

Leads
one sentence

30-35 words maximum

lead tells the most important information in the story and gives specific facts

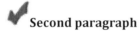
Second paragraph

expand or develop some idea introduced in the lead

should not drop the story into a chronological narrative

Attribution

All major information should be attributed unless it is commonly known or unless the information itself strongly implies the source.

Don't dump a string of direct quotations on the reader.

Direct quotations should be no more than two sentences long.

Direct quotations and their attribution should be punctuated properly.
Here's an example:
"John did not go with her," he said.

Elements of a direct quotation should be in the proper sequence, as in the example above: **direct quote, speaker, verb.**

 AP style
Always check numbers, dates, locations, titles, etc.

Check the following

pronoun-antecedent agreement

it, its, it's

"it is . . .", "there is . . .", "there are . . ." structures; avoid these. They are passive and vague.

Use the **past tense**, not the present.

Comma splice or run-on sentence, such as
He picked up the ball, he ran down the field.
Sally does not know where he is he is not here.
These are grammatically incorrect.

Plurals -- don't make them by using an "apostrophe s".

Short paragraphs -- any paragraph more than three sentences is definitely too long; any paragraph that is three sentences is probably too long.

Wordiness -- have you checked for too much verbiage, redundancies, unnecessary repetitions, etc.

Name, title -- When you put the title before a name, **do not** separate them with commas, such as
(WRONG): **Game warden, Brad Fisher, arrested the trespassers**.
When the name comes before the title, the title should be set off by

commas.

Brad Fisher, the game warden, arrested the trespassers.

✔**Transitions** -- use them to tie your paragraphs together. Don't jump from one subject to another in a new paragraph without giving the reader some warning.

✔**Don't copy** the wording of the information sheet.

✔**Names** -- check them once more to make sure they are spelled correctly.

The errors above are some of the most common that beginning writing students make in writing inverted pyramid news stories. Get into the habit of checking them on the story assignments that you get in your lab.

Headlines

Some of the most important words a journalist will write for the web are the headline. A headline has always been very important for print media. It is vitally important for the web. Because headlines appear **in lists as links** rather than with the body of the story, they are the reader's first introduction to a story. If they do not sell the reader immediately, the reader is unlikely to click on the link to go to the story.

Headlines must contain the **key words** that will convey *the subject* of the story and what the story is *about* (two different things - the first general and the second specific).

The first rule of headline writing is that the words accurately represent what is in the story. Accuracy above all else.

Headlines are abstracted sentences -- five to 10 words at most -- that convey a complete thought. That is, they must contain a subject and a verb; better yet, a subject, verb and object.

Finally, and very importantly, a good, straightforward headline is what search engines such as Google like. Headlines are the key to search engine optimization (SEO), which helps to draw traffic to a web site.

The goal: coherent information

Headline writers need to keep this question in their minds as they begin and end the process of writing the head:

If a reader were reading only your five to 10 words, would he or she know what the article is about?

The answer to that question too often is no. How many headlines have you read that left you clueless. They may contain a word or two that you understand or designate a subject that you want to read about, but they give you no real information.

WORLD »	BUSINESS »
· Mayor Declares a Coup in Madagascar	· Fisher Island: Still a Refuge, but Not From the Downturn
· As Economy Sinks, Russians Protest	· Search Service on Google Briefly Fails
· Somalis Cheer the Selection of a Moderate Islamist Cleric as President	· Preoccupations: Handing Out the Pink Slips Can Hurt, Too
U.S. »	**TECHNOLOGY »**
· A Governor's Removal Spurs (the Latest) Calls for Political Reform in Illinois	· Search Service on Google Briefly Fails
· Geithner to Unveil Strategy to Revive Credit Flow	· Novelties: 'Fantastic Voyage,' Revisited: The Pill That Navigates
· Republican Leads as a Cabinet Choice	· Unboxed: Disruptive Innovation, Applied to Health Care
POLITICS »	
· Geithner to Unveil Strategy to Revive Credit Flow	**SPORTS »**
· Republican Leads as a Cabinet Choice	· Kurt Warner, the Family Guy, Can Cement Legacy
· A Governor's Removal Spurs (the Latest) Calls for Political Reform in Illinois	· One Way or Another, Arizona's Darnell Dockett Will Get His Ink
	· Sack Specialist Smith and Woodson Join Hall
N.Y. / REGION »	**OBITUARIES »**
· For Weiner, Politics Isn't Enough of a Contact Sport	· Ingemar Johansson, Boxer, Dies at 76

Headlines, like these from the New York Times, often appear in a list by themselves. They are the only way a reader can decide whether or not the story is interesting enough to read.

Guidelines

With that question in mind, here are some guidelines.

- Headlines should be based on **the main idea of the story**. That idea should be found in the lead or introduction of the story.

- If facts are not in the story, do not use them in a headline.

- **Avoid repetition.** Don't repeat key words in the same headline; don't repeat the exact wording of the story in the headline.

- **Avoid ambiguity**, insinuations and double meanings.

- If a story qualifies a statement, the headline should also. Headline writers should understand a story completely before they write its headline. Otherwise, headlines such as the one below can occur.

- **Council to cut taxes at tonight's meeting**
- The City Council will vote on a proposal to cut property taxes by as much as 10 percent for some residents at tonight's meeting.

- The proposal, introduced two weeks ago by council member Paul Dill and backed by Mayor Pamela Frank, would offer incentives for property owners who use their property to create jobs for area residents. . .

- **Use present tense verbs** for headlines that refer to past or present events.

- For the future tense, **use the infinitive form** of the verb (such as "to go," "to run," etc.) rather than the verb "will."

- "To be" verbs, such as "is," "are," "was" and "were," should be omitted when they are used as auxiliary verbs but not as transitive verbs.

- Alliteration, if used, should be deliberate and should not go against the general tone of the story.

- **Do not use articles** — "a," "an" and "the." These take up space that could be put to better use in informing the reader. In the examples below, the second headline gives readers more information than the first.

- **New police patrols help make the streets safer**

  New patrols help make westside streets safer

- Do not use the conjunction "and." It also uses space unnecessarily. Use a comma instead.

- **Mayor and council meet on budget for next year**

  Mayor, council agree to cuts on new budget

- Avoid using unclear or little-known names, phrases and abbreviations in headlines.

- Use punctuation sparingly.

- No headline may start with a verb.

- Headlines should be complete sentences or should imply complete sentences. When a linking verb is used, it can be implied rather than spelled out.

- Avoid headlinese — that is, words such as hit, flay, rap, hike, nix, nab, slate, etc. Use words for their precise meaning.

- Do not use pronouns alone and unidentified.

- Be accurate and specific.

The original question

Keep reminding yourself of the original question we posed earlier:

If a reader were reading only your five to 10 words, would he or she know what the article is about?

Headline writing is not easy if it is done well. Some people have more facility with it than others, but anyone who is determined to be a journalist can lean to write a good headline.

Audio and video journalism:
Writing to be heard and seen

Most of what you hear on radio and television is written.

TV and radio are word media, even though video and sounds often drive a story. The words and meanings must be clear.

The web has added a dimension to audio (and video) that we have never had before. We can now use sounds in a different way, and we are not confined to the formats or practices that were developed for radio.

For example, a story might have this quote:

"I saw the crash from a distance — maybe 50 or 60 yards — but it was terrible," she said.

But you could include an audio clip with your story, and it is this:

You can hear this audio clip at the following URL:
http://intercollegiatenews.com/jem200/files/2011/07/crash-quote.mp3

Does that sound clip convey a different meaning than the one you got when you read it?

Or, take this example:

For an amateur, Smith has the guitar techniques of a professional with many years of experience. Here's a sample of his work (:40):

You can hear this audio clip at the following URL:
http://intercollegiatenews.com/jem200/files/2011/07/Smith-guitar.mp3

Journalists need to learn how to take advantage of these new ways of communicating.

Every journalists must be well-schooled in recording and editing audio.

Writing for audio

When you are writing for audio, with it is a news story or an introduction to someone else, the writing

– must be clear

– must be for the ear (to be heard, not read), which means

- short words
- short sentences, one idea or fact per sentence
- simple sentence structure
  SUBJECT > VERB > PREDICATE > PERIOD
- pronounceable words
- use of contractions
- casual but not informal
- efficient – make every word count
- active voice

– must be written to time – how long does it take to say it

– must be written to be spoken

Learning to speak/record audio journalism (yourself)

Part of audio journalism means you have to learn to do it – that is, to speak it.

– using proper English

– speaking in complete sentences, complete thoughts•

– clarity (enunciation)

– logic (coherence)

– pace – speaking slowly enough to be understood, fast enough to be interesting

– practice, practice, practice (seriously)

– speaking with confidence, eliminating uhs, y'knows and that other word

Clarity, clarity, clarity

Above all else, you must learn to speak in a way that people hear what you're saying and understand it. Learn not to speak so slowly that you are boring or so quickly that listeners don't hear the words and syllables.

Personality

And after you get some practice and confidence, learn to insert some personality into your recordings by varying the **tone** and **inflection**.

Dramatic unity

Remember, the key to all good writing for the mass media is to understand what you are writing about. Broadcast writing is no different. The writer has to understand thoroughly the information that must be presented. Then the writer has to begin asking some questions:

* What is the dominant theme?

* What facts illuminate or help develop this theme?

* What is the principal impression I want to leave with the viewer?

* What is the most significant or interesting part of this story?

* What is necessary for understanding this story?

* What can I leave out?

The major structure of writing that we will learn for audio and video journalism is called dramatic unity. That is a structure that allows us to tell a story quickly and without a lot of detail.

The dramatic unity structure has three parts: climax, cause and effect. The structure is usually represented by a circle, symbolizing the fact that all of these parts are necessary for a good story. (Remember when we talked about the inverted pyramid structure? We said that some of the least important information might be eliminated. That's not the case with dramatic unity. You don't eliminate any part of it.)

- **Climax** – the end of the story; the most important thing that happened; the most dramatic thing that happened. That comes first.
- **Cause** – why did it happen? what are the circumstances under which it occurred? what are the facts that can illuminate the climax and help the reader understand what happened and why?
- **Effect** – explain the outcome, the effect or the future of the event; try to bring this story to a satisfying conclusion.

Take a look at the example on the right. You should note several major differences in writing style from what we have previously practiced in this course. What are some of those? What else do you see in this story that we have not discussed yet?

Writing the audio news story

Climax — what is most important or dramatic of the story? Remember when we talked about news writing, we discussed things that should almost always be in a lead paragraph or near the top of a story: people killed or injured, property damage, large numbers of people affected by an event, etc. The same thing — and many of the same rules — apply to broadcast writing.

The city has delayed a seven hundred thousand dollar drainage project in the Coventry and Lakeshore Drive areas. City officials say they need approval for the project from the Army Corps of Engineers.

Cause — what are the facts that will expand or develop the climax of the story? In this sense, "cause" doesn't necessarily mean what caused the event. Rather, it means what can you say that will help the listener to understand the event better. For instance, in the example below — the next part of the story begun above — what is said is not the "cause," but it does help the listener to understand this story better.

The city has planned this project for months without knowing it needed Corps approval. But today the city engineer announced that federal regulations require plans be submitted to the Corps.

Effect — what information can bring this story to a conclusion? Again, we are not necessarily talking about an "effect" in the sense of cause-and-effect. We are simply looking for a way to bring the story to a conclusion.

That action could delay the project for six months. Residents say they are surprised and disappointed that the work won't begin soon.

This was a difficult story to write. It was a story that had a lot of complexity and detail that could not be included. For instance, the residents had been waiting for several years to have this work down. While that was implied in the story, it could not be explicitly stated. Another thing that the story leaves out is why the city is suddenly finding out that the Corps of Engineers has to approve a project.

This story could be improved in several ways. Look at the last sentence. It contains five (count 'em, five) sibilants — residents, say, surprised, disappointed, soon. Some of these words may be necessary, or they may not have good substitutes. Still, this story could use some judicious editing and even rewriting.

Here are a couple of other stories. See if they are any better.

Climax

Chicago police are looking into the death early Tuesday morning of 72-year-old Mary Ryan at the California Gardens Nursing Center in Little Village.

Cause

Ryan reportedly received a morphine injection from her 38-year-old daughter just hours before her death. Ryan was suffering from numerous terminal illnesses.

Effect

The case is just a death investigation at this time.

Climax

An Illinois state trooper was killed in a fiery car crash in Downers Grove overnight.

Cause

The trooper was 29-year-old Chung Lin. The driver of the pickup truck that rear-ended the trooper, Azaria (a-ZAR-ee-A) Maja (Ma-JA), has been charged with reckless driving.

Effect

He is in the hospital in fair condition with lacerations to his face. Three other people suffered minor injuries.

Using the present context

Some students don't completely understand when they should use the present tense in writing broadcast news. (Some don't understand what the present tense is — sometimes. Make sure you know.)

The present tense is a good way to introduce a sense of immediacy into your copy. Even though you are writing about things that have already happened, expressing them in the present tense rather than the past tense helps the writer lay stress immediacy.

Here are a few guidelines about using the present tense in broadcast copy:

* when the action is continuing

Hurricane Sally is battering the New England coast today.

The governor plans a special session of the legislature next month

* when the action is in the immediate past and has some continuing effect

The president says he will veto the budget bill.

* when referring to something in the future

The Kroger company has announced that it is closing its stores in the city.

* but not when it is clearly inappropriate.

Two people are killed in a three-car accident last night on I-59.

Video journalism

Every story begins with an idea.

The idea then coalesces into something smaller and more practical. Something doable.

At some point in the process – sooner is better than later – the idea is condensed into a single sentence, so that if someone asked you, "What story are you working on right now?" you could tell that person in a single sentence and without hesitating.

If you can do that, chances are your idea is a good one and you will be able to produce a good video story.

If your story idea is still at the stage that you take several sentences to explain it, chances are you are not going to be able to produce it easily or coherently. Or you are going to spend a lot of time doing things that are not necessary. Or both.

So, Rule Number One: Get the story idea together.

Rule Number One-A: Keep it simple.

Once you get the idea (one sentence – no more), then start asking the journalistic questions:

• Who. Who is involved in the story? What one or two people do I need to talk to? Can I get to them? Will they talk to me?

• What. What is the central piece of action or the central idea – the one thing on which the story is centered? Can I get a picture of it? Better yet, can I shoot video of it? How can I capture that with a video camera?

• Where. The location of the story is of prime importance. As a video journalist, you are going to have to go there. It's not likely that it will come to you. So, you ask: Can I get there? Can I take a camera? Is it a place where I can shoot video so that it will mean something to the people who watch the story?

• When. What is the time element of this story? Is it an event? Or is it an idea? Will it be gone tomorrow, or can the story wait for a day or a week? The last question does not mean you should consider procrastinating. It simply helps you with your planning.

When you get answers to those questions, you are beginning to think like a journalist.

But you are just beginning.

Now you should begin forming an outline for the story – a mental storyboard. You make some phone calls or send some emails. (If you are working on a story that will be broadcast that day, you make phone calls. Email – even texting – is too slow.) You ask people for information. You begin gathering facts, information, impressions. You get an idea of where the story is headed based on what you find out. Sometimes, your original central idea is confirmed. Sometimes it isn't. You have to adjust.

As the story begins to take shape in your head, you consider what you need to be telling and what you can show: interviews, action scenes, still pictures, pan shots, etc.

You set up interviews, and you go to where the sources are. You go to the scene of the event or story idea, if there is one. You are constantly thinking – constantly asking yourself: How can I tell this story? What do I need – an interview with Person A, a shot of Place B, etc.

Finally, when you have shot the video you think you need, you sit down to write. Unless it's breaking news and you're covering the event live, your story won't really come together until you have written it. And without good writing, your story won't be worth watching.

So you think about the arc of the story – the introduction, what bits go in the middle, the way it ends. What is the video that you want to use? Does it need an intro? Does it need a voice over? Are all these things related to the central idea of the story as you first defined it or as you adjusted it during your reporting?

Does the story hang together? Does the video support the writing?

Can the way you're telling the story be understood by a viewer who knows little or nothing about the story? Is it clear from the very beginning to the very end?

These are hard questions, but they are the ones the good video journalist asks again and again throughout the time that the story is being produced, all the while working under two extraordinarily difficult strictures:

Get it right.

Keep it simple.

Shooting the video

The camera does not speak. It does not tell the story. It is held, aimed, pointed, positioned.

The person holding the camera – the videographer is the professional term – is the story-teller.

The story is in the head of the journalist, who in many cases is the videographer as well as the writer and producer. The camera is simply the tool the journalist/videographer uses to get the story to the viewer.

How does that happen?

Here are some basic things that everyone who uses a video camera should know:

• **Plan and think.** The most important tool the video journalist has is not a camera. It's the brain. As much as possible, video journalists should find out what information they can about the story they are shooting, who's involved, where it's located and what will happen. They should know before they arrive on the scene the people they want to talk with and the kinds of shots they want to make.

In addition, they should also size up a situation quickly, hold the camera up and shoot the interesting things that happen right in front of them. Video journalists should shoot efficiently, but they should err on the side of having too much video rather than too little.

• **Framing.** The concept of framing simply means understanding what will look good when you turn the camera on and what won't. One of the rules of framing is to "fill the frame." That is, when you are shooting, you should not have much "margin" around the subject, if any at all. Generally, the closer you are to the subject, the better your shots and your framing will be. Another concept of framing is to apply the rule of thirds to the video camera. The rule of thirds is an imaginary set of horizontal lines that divide what you see in the viewfinder into three equal parts and an imaginary set of vital lines that do the same thing. Taken together, the picture is divided into nine parts. Seeing the picture divided like this helps in a number of ways. For one, if the picture is of someone's face, the person's eyes should be along the top horizontal line. Getting a center of interest at one of the four points where the lines intersect is also a useful technique.

Head room is another term you will hear in a discussion of framing. This refers to the space in a head shot between the top of the head and the top of the picture. Generally, there should be some space for head room, but sometimes filling the picture with the head – or even cutting off the top of the head – may be appropriate for the story.

• **Holding the camera.** Sometimes you will need to hold the camera. Sometimes you will use a tripod. Whichever you do, you will need to keep the camera steady. If you are holding the camera, this will require practice and getting comfortable with the camera itself. Holding the camera with your elbows against your ribs is one technique for keeping the camera steady. Another is to put your elbows on a stable surface like a table. A tripod solves the problem of making sure the camera is steady, but it also immobilizes the camera so that it can be used in only one spot – or it can be moved along with the tripod.

• **Camera angles and shots.** Try to get a variety of angles and shots whenever you use your video camera. Used judiciously, different types of shots will make the story more interesting for the viewer. (Check out this page on MediaCollege.com http://www.mediacollege.com/video/shots/ for examples of the different types of shots you can use.) Resist turning the camera so that the picture is angled. This is disorienting for the viewer and quickly becomes irritating, and you are likely to lose viewers if you do this without good reason.

Watch this video on TV news scripting by Prof. Mark Harmon and his class. The video demonstrates the various kinds of scripts and how they are built. The video is at http://youtu.be/cQWke4zxv3w.

116

The best way to learn any of this, of course, is to go out and do it. Cover stories, shoot action, interview people. Carry your camera and be ready to use it. As a video journalist, you should follow two basic rules:

• **Shoot a lot.** Get different kinds of shots. Follow the 10-second rule of turning the camera on 10 seconds before you ask the first question and leaving it running for 10 seconds after you finish. (You'll find you need this space when you edit your video.)

• **Carry a pen and notebook.** Don't depend on your memory. Write things down, particularly names and titles of people. Take notes during interviews or during shooting if your camera is on a tripod.

Terms

information	objectivity	audio
timeliness	fairness	video
modesty	deadline	inflection
immediacy	audience	dramatic unity
interactivity	transitions	present context
linkage	inverted pyramid	angle
mobility	lead	framing
inform	Four Horsemen	
persuade	headline	
entertain	key words	

The First Amendment

The First Amendment to the U.S. Constitution protects five important freedoms: religion, speech, press, assembly and petition. Even though the First Amendment has been in the Constitution for almost the entire history of the republic, the idea of its protective powers has been slow to develop.

Religion

Many Americans have their history wrong. They believe that the first European settlers of this nation came to America because they believed in the right to practice religion and worship freely.

Actually, many of them came because they wanted to practice their religion freely. They did not care about the right of people outside their own groups to observe a different set of beliefs.

During the colonial years there was a much religious intolerance and state supported religion practice as there was in England or any place else in Europe.

But that began to change in the late 18th century, particularly through the writing and efforts of Thomas Jefferson, who challenged the government's role in religious observance.

Freedom of religion today

Today, through many events and court cases, we have developed some fundamental understandings about what the words of the First Amendment mean (sometimes referred to as the 'establishment clause'):

Individuals have the right to believe, practice religion, and worship as they see fit.

Individuals are not required to support any religion or religious organization.

The government cannot establish or support any religious organization.

The government must remain neutral in dealing with religious organizations and beliefs.

Even with these fundamental understandings, there are still many controversies and issues surrounding the First Amendment's guarantee of freedom of religion and of the state neutrality toward religion. For instance, consider these:

– prayer in schools

– creationism

– posting the Ten Commandments in government buildings

– requiring the recitation of the Pledge of Allegiance in schools

– blue laws

– putting Christmas decorations on public property

The list could go on.

Speech

If the First Amendment means anything, we believe, it means that we have the right to speak our minds — to say what we think, right?

That's correct.

But it wasn't always so.

In the early days of the republic, laws were passed that protected the president and administration from criticism.

Many states had laws restricting the freedom of speech, especially in the South where is was against the law to advocate abolition (freeing slaves). Yet Americans have always enjoyed debating the issues of the day. They like to argue, disagree, and even diss one another. From colonial days Americans have sought solutions to social, economic and political problems by vigorous and animated discussion. Sometimes those discussions have turned violent. More often than not, however, the discussions have ultimately resulted in commonly agreed upon solutions and principles.

Despite its halting beginning, "free speech" proved its value more than once, and the concept is now deeply embedded in the American psyche.

Still, as much as we honor free speech, we are sometimes not very careful in preserving it. Our tendency to censor speech that is disturbing or disagreeable -- or that doesn't agree with what seems to be the majority opinion -- sometimes gets the best of us. We also have a tendency to think that if we limit speech in certain ways and on certain topics, we can solve some pressing social problem. Particularly during national crises, we tend to believe that if we can just stop people from saying certain things, our nation will be more secure.

When we do this, however, we are defying our own best instincts and a logic that experience teaches again and again. We can never successfully keep people from saying what they believe in, from believing whatever they choose, and from expressing those beliefs publicly. Other societies try doing this, and eventually they explode.

People do not like to be told that they cannot say something.

Neither do we.

Our job as Americans is to protect free speech wherever it is threatened. We should constantly be on guard against the thinking that restricting speech will somehow make us a better society. We should preserve our unique place in the world as a society who values its individual citizens and protects them even when they say or do things that are not popular.

Press

This part of the First Amendment

'... or *of the press ...*'

has generated a great deal of debate and much litigation throughout the history of the republic.

Just what did the founders of the Republic mean by that? How have we interpreted that phrase since it was originally written?

Answers to those questions have filled many volumes, but generally we believe that the government should not censor printed material; that it should not exercise prior restraint (preventing something from being printed or distributed) on publications; and that it should not hinder the distribution of printed material.

In journalism, this freedom extends to the practice of journalism itself. Reporters should be able to gather information. Government bodies –

courts, legislative units, boards, etc. – should operate in the open. Government records should be available to all citizens who request them. In some cases, reporters are protected from disclosing their sources because of this clause in the First Amendment.

Two important areas where the freedom to publish is limited are: libel or defamation; and copyright and trademark.

Libel or defamation

Libel – the concept that words can harm a person's reputation – is an ancient principle of common law. A person's reputation has value, and when that value is diminished, a person can see redress from the courts.

Yet there is the First Amendment, which says society has value in being able to speak freely. How do we resolve this conflict?

Despite the language of the First Amendment, libel laws exist and are, occasionally, enforced. Journalists must be careful about libel.

Modern defamation laws say that to win a libel case, you must prove

• publication (more than just two people have to see/hear it)

• identification (can the person defamed be identified)

• defamation (did the words have potential to do real damage)

• fault (was there negligence or some mitigation)

harm (is there provable damage)

Defenses against defamation

Statute and case law provide some strong defenses for people facing libel actions:

• truth – powerful defense (society values truth)

• qualified privilege – is the situation one that relieves people of libel responsibility? Reporters depend on the concept of qualified privilege to report public affairs. For instance, they may report the arrest of a person who is ultimately is declared innocent of a crime.

• absolute privilege – Some instances, such as a legislator speaking in a meeting of the legislature, can say anything he or she wishes without regard to libel laws.

• statute of limitations – Courts do not like old cases, particularly in civil matters. Many states have a statue of limitations provision that says a libel suit must be filed within two years of the alleged libel.

• Constitutional privilege – This privilege protects news media from suits by public officials and public figures. It comes from a 1964 decision, New York Times v Sullivan. The results of this case make virtually impossible for any well known figure to recover damages in a libel action.

Still, the threat of the costs of litigation are real, and journalists should be careful to avoid them if possible.

Copyright

The freedom to write and publish is not unlimited.

One area in which that freedom is limited is that of copyright and trademarks, which are part of a larger area of law known as intellectual property. People who create what we might term generally as "intellectual property" – books, musical works, art, sculpture, articles, poems, etc. – have some protection in the way that those works are used by others. If you draw a picture or write a poem, that picture or poem is yours (at least for a limited amount of time), and no one else can reprint it without your permission.

There are things that copyright does not cover, however.

Facts cannot be copyrighted. Let's say you are the only writer covering your high school basketball game, and you write a story about it for the high school paper. Another publication can take the facts that you have described – the details of the game, the score, etc. – and use them in its description of the game.

That publication, however, cannot use your account of the game. The expression of facts can be copyrighted, but the facts themselves cannot.

Like facts, ideas cannot be copyrighted, but the expression of those ideas can. For instance, you can paint a picture of a tree, and that painting will be copyrighted. Someone else can paint a picture of the same tree. That's ok, as long as they do not use your painting.

The protection of a copyright is limited in two important ways. One is that it does not last forever. Currently, copyrights last for the life of the creator, plus 70 years. If the copyright is owned by a corporation, the copyright lasts longer. A copyright does not last forever. At some point, all creative works become part of the "public domain"; that is, everyone owns them. Consequently, the works of William Shakespeare, for instance, are in the public domain, and Shakespeare can be quoted at length without anyone's permission.

The second limitation of copyright is through the concept of fair use. This concept has been developed to encourage the dissemination of ideas and information without either putting a great burden on the user or infringing on the rights of the creator of the work. Fair use means that in certain limited circumstances, a copyrighted work – or more likely, some portion of it – may be used without the permission of the holder of the copyright.

Courts have looked at four things in considering what is fair use:

– the nature of the copyrighted material – how much effort it took to produce it;

– the nature of the use – for instance, material used in an educational setting for educational purposes is more likely to be thought of as fair use;

– the extent of the use – how much of the copyrighted material is used, just a few words or a whole passage;

– commercial infringement – most importantly, how much does the use hurt the commercial value of the work.

Unless material is being used in a very limited way, you should always get permission to use copyrighted material. Holders of copyright can be very aggressive about enforcing their copyrights, and the unauthorized user of a copyright can be fined substantially. Many people in education believe that they can use any material in any way they wish, and it will be considered fair use. That is not the case. Educators are bound by copyright laws as much as anyone else.

Note: Material on the Internet has as much copyright protection as anything else. Some people believe that whatever is on a web site is in the public domain, and that is not the case. Just because material is easy to access does not mean that it does not have copyright protection.

Trademark

A special protection for the commercial use of words, phrases and symbols is trademark.

Many companies go to great lengths to protect their trademarks because that is how the public identifies their products. What if, for example, a shoe company named Nuke started using the Nike symbol, the swoosh, on its shoes? Consumers might become confused about what product to buy, and Nike, which holds a trademark on the swoosh, might be hurt by that.

Assembly

The First Amendment guarantees that people can get together – peaceably – and talk about whatever they want to discuss.

Courts have almost always recognized that governments have the power to regulate time and place of assembly when the public's safety and convenience is an issue.

But governments are prevented from saying to a group of people that they cannot meet when the reason for their meeting is legal.

According to the First Amendment Center:

First Amendment freedoms ring hollow if government officials can repress expression that they fear will create a disturbance or offend. Unless there is real danger of imminent harm, assembly rights must be respected.

About the picture:

Before 1920, most women in the United States could not vote. In the 19th century, they had few legal rights at all, and the social customs against women being seen in public unless they were with another woman or accompanied by a man were strict and unacceptable by today's standards. When women starting petitioning for the right to vote in the early part of the 20th century, they began holding parades, exercising their right to assembly. Here is the beginning of the Washington Suffrage Parade of 1913, a significant event in the history of the suffrage movement. For more information on this parade and its effect on the eventual passage of the Nineteenth Amendment, go to Seeing Suffrage.

Petition

When an individual

• calls the tax assessor's office to complain that property taxes have gone up too much,

• attends a town meeting public officials and policies are questioned,

• joins a legal street demonstration to gain publicity for their cause,

• pays a lobbyist or joins a group that pays someone to go to Washington or the state capital to argue for a cause,

then that person is petitioning 'the Government for a redress of grievances' – a right protected by the First Amendment.

The right to petition the government was very much on the minds of the Founding Fathers. As colonists, they had asked King George III and the government in London many times to pay attention to what they wanted. Mostly, the people in England ignored them.

So, when it came time to write the Declaration of Independence, they included the following in their reasons for declaring independence:

In every state of these Oppressions We have Petitioned for Redress in the most humble terms: Our repeated Petitions have been answered only by repeated injury.

Governments in the U.S. do not have to agree with the petitioner or do what he or she asks. But they must listen.

And they cannot retaliate against the petitioner for asking.

Compared to the other parts of the First Amendment, the right to petition the government has not generated much litigation or attention among scholars over the years. Perhaps, according to Adam Newton, writing for the First Amendment Center, that is because it continues to work so well. The petition clause is the tacit assumption in constitutional analysis, the primordial right from which other expressive freedoms arise. Why speak, why publish, why assemble against the government at all if such complaints will only be silenced?

About the picture:

Mary Gertrude Fendall (left) and Mary Dubrow (right) standing outside what is likely National Woman's Party headquarters, holding between them a large sign containing text of a Resolution Addressed to Senator Edward J. Gay with a long unrolled sheet of paper, presumably signatures on a petition, laying on the ground in front of them. The sign was in support of the Nineteenth Amendment, which would given women the right to vote. The sign mentions mentions that "President Woodrow Wilson has urged the passage of the Federal Suffrage amendment before the Senate of the United States and again recently before the whole Congress of the United States as a necessary War and Reconstruction Measure . . ." Wilson first publicly declared his support for the amendment on Jan. 9, 1918. He asked the Senate to pass the amendment as a war measure on Sept. 30, 1918. The amendment was passed in the House on May 21, 1919, and in the Senate on June 4, 1919. Library of Congress photos, circa 1918-1919.

History

First Amendment Videos

Gitlow v. New York

Videos of Dr. Dwight Teeter discussing various aspects of the First Amendment and how it developed can be found at these links:

https://vimeo.com/9852487

https://vimeo.com/9754284

https://vimeo.com/9748541

https://vimeo.com/9823451

https://vimeo.com/9772215

The First Amendment grew our of four concepts of behavior of human beings in society (as identified by Teeter, Le Duc, and Loving):

- marketplace of ideas

- individual fulfillment

- safety valve

- self-governance

Each of the concepts is important for an understanding of why people in the 18th century -- the time when America earned its independence from Great Britain and adopted the Constitution -- believed in the notion of freedom of speech.

The marketplace of ideas is based on the concept that no one person or entity knows the truth that can be applied to every action of mankind. Since no human has the authority to say what is right or wrong or true or not true, ideas must be expressed and tested. The famous English author John Milton gave voice to the marketplace of ideas (although he did not use that term), and many in the 18th century followed his line of thinking. Simply put, the concept is that if everyone can express his or her ideas, the truth will eventually emerge.

Individual fulfillment means that all people have potential to become more than they area. As humans, they need the freedom to express themselves and to try to expand and improve their character and productivity. By doing this, they are of benefit to the entire society. People can define themselves through their individual expressions.

The idea of freedom of speech as a safety valve means that individuals can express opposition to authority without punishment, and this -- in the long run -- has a calming effect on the political society. If people know that at the very least they can speak and be heard, they are less likely to rebel against the whole structure of the state.

Finally, free speech is the basis of self governance. No society can claim to have its people self governing if it does not allow free expression of ideas.

These ideas were floating around and much debate when America won its independence from Great Britain in the 1780s. A great deal of free speech had already been practiced by the Founding Fathers as they were making war against Britain and as they were setting up their own government, so individual rights did not seem like a critical issue.

But as Americans debated the ratification of a new Constitution in 1787 and 1788, many prominent people -- people such as Patrick Henry and Samuel Adams -- opposed the Constitution because they believed that it would concentrate too much power in the hands of two few people. Individual liberties -- the right to speak and to assemble, for instance -- would be threatened by the newly powerful centralized authorities.

To counter those arguments, proponents of the Constitution promised that, once the document was ratified and put into place, they would support a set of amendments that would guarantee the rights about which the opponents were concerned. James Madison, who had been a chief architect of the Constitution itself, took the lead in drafting these amendments, which eventually became known as the Bill of Rights.

The First Amendment is the first of 10 of these amendments. Some deal with individual liberties. Others deal with how the government much handle individuals accused of a crime. Still others restrict government action in certain areas.

The First Amendment is not first because the Founding Fathers considered it the most important one. The historical record indicates that they clearly did not. Still, the fact that it is first has invested it with much value. What is means exactly is still a matter of vigorous debate.

The politics of the First Amendment

The First Amendment, as Professor Teeter says in the video in the previous section, is "the chance product of political expediency." (He's quoting Leonard Levy, another First Amendment scholar.) How did that happen?

James Madison was the chief author of the new Constitution that had been put forth by those wanting to form a strong central government in 1787. As such, Madison became one of the leaders in arguing for its ratification. The Constitution was the product of weeks of delicate compromise on many of its points, and Madison feared that any changes to it would destroy its chance for passage.

That's exactly what the opponents of the Constitution hoped, and they began complaining that the Constitution did not protect individuals from the powers of government to take away civil liberties, such as freedom of speech, freedom of the press and the right to trial by jury. This debate took place in just about every state that considered the Constitution but it was conducted fiercely in Virginia, Madison's home state. Opponents were led by Patrick Henry, the popular orator of the Revolution and a man still active in politics. Henry and other feared a powerful central government.

Sitting on the fence in this debate were the Virginia Baptists and other religious groups who had been fighting against the established and official religion of the Anglican church. Baptists were persuaded by these argument -- especially by the lack of separation of church and state.

This put them and James Madison in an awkward position. Madison and the Baptists had been strong allies in the fight against an established church. Now, Madison appeared to be abandoning that principle with his support for this new Constitution.

In truth, Madison did not think that these rights needed to be protected by the new Constitution, and he feared that adding them would upset the fine balance he had struck to complete the Constitution to begin with. But recognized and understood the concerns of his friends, the Baptists. He also knew that without their support, it would be unlikely that Virginia would ratify the Constitution. And if Virginia, the largest state among the original 13 colonies, did not do so, the Constitution itself would not be ratified.

So, Madison promised to support a bill of rights that would be added to the Constitution after it had been ratified and the first government had been established. He promised to run for Congress and then to do what he could to introduce the necessary amendments. That stance put Madison in the position of admitting that there was something lacking about the Constitution that he so ardently supported. Still, he did want was necessary and was able to persuade the Baptists and other concerned religious groups to his side.

The Constitution was ultimately ratified, and the new government was put in place.

Madison was elected to the Congress but initially found little support among his colleagues for immediately amending the Constitution before it had had a chance to work. Still, he had made a promise, and he used his massive intellect and political skill to keep that promise

As historian Forrest Church has written:

His (Madison's) authorship of the First Amendment constitutes perhaps his most abiding legacy. Acting on the crucial impetus provided by his Baptist constituents, he etched church-state separate and freedom of conscience into the American code.

For more on the ratification battles over the U.S. Constitution, see the Teaching American History website.

The First Amendment in the 19th and early 20th centuries

By the early 1790s, the First Amendment, along with the other nine amendments that constituted the Bill of Rights, had been ratified -- and seemingly quickly forgotten. During the single term of the John Adams presidency (1797 - 1800), Congress passed and the president signed the Alien and Sedition Acts that outlawed criticism of the president and those in power. (Figure -.-)

Republicans such as Thomas Jefferson and James Madison -- in opposition to the Federalists -- could do little about these acts. The Supreme Court had not yet established itself as the body that could review laws passed by Congress for their constitutionality, so there was at that point no check on congressional power. The acts themselves were ineffective in stifling criticism of the president, and fortunately, they expired after two years. By that time, Thomas Jefferson had been elected president, and the Federalists would never return to power. The Alien and Sedition Acts stained the Adams presidency, and they made heroes out of those they meant to persecute.

The First Amendment and the other parts of the Bill of Rights were meant to restrain Congress. People of the early republic saw their power and intent as limited. States and state constitutions were still the source of governmental power that Americans recognized as most important. Recall that the First Amendment begins with the words: "Congress shall make no law . . ." This phrase was deliberate and taken seriously by the people of the time. Congress could not make laws, but states certainly could.

In addition, we need to understand that the greatest concern of those who composed the First Amendment was religious liberty and the free exercise of religious practices -- not free expression. Madison, Jefferson and their allies wanted to prevent the new government from establishing an official church -- not guaranteeing free speech or a free press. They wanted to build a "wall of separation" between the government and the church.

In this, they were highly successful. Religious liberty and the free exercise of religion -- without interference from the government became an established principle of the nation. It is one that remains in effect today, so much so that we often take it for granted.

But the idea of freedom of expression had a tougher time.

The chief and abiding political and moral issue facing American in the first half of the 19th century was slavery. Slave had been in America for 300 years by that time, and slavery had worked its way into the social, political and economic system. As tobacco and cotton -- particularly cotton -- grew in importance, slavery as a means of producing these products also strengthened.

The emotional and political costs were enormous.

Whites, especially those in the South where slavery existed and grew, lived in constant fear that slaves would one day rise up in bloody revolt. Those fears were not groundless. Slaves in the newly formed nation of Haiti had done just that, and every Southern plantation resident had nightmares that the same thing would happen on their land, even though they might fool themselves into thinking that their slaves were happy and contented.

Northerners shared many of those fears, and because their economic systems did not depend so much of cotton and tobacco, Northern states were able to free themselves slowly from the slavery system. Still, the fear of the possibility of a slave revolt was national.

Consequently, those who advocated freedom for slaves --emancipationists and abolitionists -- were not welcome in many places. Southern states passed laws against the printing and distribution of abolitionist newspapers. They also outlawed the open advocacy of emancipation or abolition. In some cases, newspaper editors who wrote about such things had their presses destroyed, were run out of town, or in a few tragic instances killed. Clearly, these situations offend our 21st century ideas of what the First Amendment should mean, but most people of the time did not view the First Amendment in this fashion.

One man who did was a Kentucky newspaper editor named Cassius Marcellus Clay. Clay had come from a slave-holding family in Kentucky but during his college days at Yale had been persuaded that slavery was wrong. He became an emancipationist, someone who advocated the gradual freeing of slaves. (Abolitionists favored immediate freedom for slaves.) Clay was stubborn and tough. He was criticized harshly for his stance and physically attacked several times for what he wrote about slavery.

Clay was one of the few men of the 19th century to say that the First Amendment to the Constitution should protect people like him from any government intrusion.

The nation did not hear or heed Clay, and those who advocated unpopular ideas were subjected to legal and extra-legal pressures to conform or remain silent. During the Civil War, Lincoln and his administration brought government power to bear against those they felt were endangering the war efforts.

The one bright spot in the 19th century for civil liberties came in 1868 when the nation ratified the 14th Amendment, which said that states could not deprive people of liberty or proper without resorting to "due process of law" and could not deny people the "equal protection" of the law. This amendment was put in place to assure that freed slaves would be given their full rights in states where slavery has previously be prevalent. This was clearly a check on state power and an assertion that the U.S. Constitution was the ultimate law of the land. It was another 50 years before this idea -- that states had to be subject to the will of the federal constitution -- took hold in any meaningful sense. When it did, in a 1925 Supreme Court ruling, it changed the entire balance of legal power in the United States and set us on the road to our modern thinking about First Amendment protections.

Meanwhile, America endured several national crises, including what was then known as the Great War (1914 - 1918). We call it World War I today. It was a time, more than any other in the nation's history, when the American government, under the direction of Woodrow Wilson, strayed from the principle of protecting free expression.

In 1917, the year America entered the war, Congress passed the Espionage Act which made it a crime "to willfully cause or attempt to cause insubordination, disloyalty, mutiny, or refusal of duty, in the military or naval forces of the United States," or to "willfully obstruct the recruiting or enlistment service of the United States."

The next year saw passage of the Sedition Act, which outlawed spoken or printed criticism of the U.S. government, the Constitution or the flag.

The Wilson administration was vigorous in using these laws and other means to suppress dissent. Part of the woman suffrage movement -- the Woman Political Party led by Alice Paul -- were particularly irritating to the administration. Despite America's entry into the war, members of the NWP continued to picket the White House, demanding that Wilson support suffrage at home while he was touting the expansion of democracy abroad.

The women picketers were arrested for "obstructing sidewalk traffic" and hauled off to jail. At first, their sentences were relatively light (two to six days in many cases), and the administration hoped the arrests would discourage future demonstrations. The opposite occurred.

Women continued to picket the White House, and the signs they carried grew more pointed. When they were rearrested, they were given longer sentences. The women asked to be treated as political prisoners, a status they were denied. They then we on hunger strikes. Prison officials, with the administration's approval, subjected the women the women to forced feeding, a torture process that kept the women alive but weakened and injured them.

Once out of jail, the suffragists continued to picket the White House and tell the story of what happened to them at the hands of government officials -- all for non-violently demanding their political rights. The picketing and protests continued after the war and up until the passage of the 19th Amendment that gave women the right to vote.

The treatment the suffragists received was not as harsh that meted out to those charged and convicted under the Espionage and Sedition Acts. Some people spend years in prison for the crime of protesting the nation's involvement in the Great War -- violating the rights to speech and petition that the First Amendment was supposed to protect.

Courts were of little use in protecting these rights. The Supreme Court on numerous occasions had the opportunity to check the administration's actions but failed to do so.

As America came out of the war, many people were disturbed by the heavy-handedness of the Wilson administration in suppressing dissent. They believed that America was in danger of losing its way as the beacon of free societies and that more attention should be paid to actively protecting civil liberties than to simply saying that "Congress shall make no law . . ."

This change in attitude did not occur all at once. Rather, it was a step-by-step process that began with the Supreme Court ruling in Gitlow v. New

York in 1925. In that decision, for the first time, the Court said that because of the 14th Amendment, Constitutional protections, such as those in the First Amendment, applied to state actions. This decision opened the door for a wide variety of other decisions during the next 40 years that strengthened protections guaranteed by the Bill of Rights.

Some final words

Writing, in the words of writing guru William Zinsser, is a process, not a product. People serious about the process are continually examining and re-examining what they do. They are explorers. This chapter contains some essays written by the author exploring writing.

ESSAY: Saving the Revolution

George Washington, winter of 1776; army in winter quarters at Valley Forge.

Washington needed to keep the army together at all costs.

But cold and lack of provisions made the men think about going home.

Right at that time, Thomas Paine wrote and published a pamphlet called The American Crisis. Washington thought so much of what Paine had written that he had it read aloud to his men.

Here's how it starts:

These are the times that try men's souls: The summer soldier and the sunshine patriot will, in this crisis, shrink from the service of their country; but he that stands it now, deserves the love and thanks of man and woman. Tyranny, like hell, is not easily conquered; yet we have this consolation with us, that the harder the conflict, the more glorious the triumph.

Washington always credited Paine for boosting the confidence and moral of his men.

Simple, powerful words. They changed minds and changed lives.

ESSAY: A high school journalist goes undercover

David McSwane wanted to do something unusual, "something cool."

What he did was a story for his high school newspaper that made the U.S. Army pay attention and shut down their recruiting efforts for a day while all Army recruiters attended ethics classes.

McSwane is a senior at Arvada West High School in Colorado. He had heard that the Army was having trouble recruiting because of the increasing unpopularity of the war in Iraq, and he had seen recruiters at his high school. It occurred to him to test out how far the recruiters would go to get somebody to sign up.

"I wanted to do something cool, go undercover and do something unusual," he told the Rocky Mountain News. (Much of the information here comes from the RMN story published this week about him. Here is a link to the RMN's April 30, 2005 story about McSwane.)

McSwane showed up at the Army recruiting office in Golden, Colo., posing as a high school dropout and describing himself as addicted to marijuana and "psychedelic muchrooms." He acted spaced out, stoned and stupid.

None of that seemed to matter to the recruiters, he said. They told him that his addiction could be licked, and when he said he couldn't do it, they told him that he could buy a detox kit that would "clean you out." One recruiter even offered to pay for half of the cost of the kit. The recruiters drove him to a local head shop so he could buy the kit.

The lack of a high school diploma didn't bother the recruiters either. They encouraged him to take a high school equivalency diploma exam. McSwane took the test but deliberately failed it. (In real life, McSwane is an honors student at Arvada West.) Again, none of this seems to be a problem for the recruiters.

McSwane was told that he could exercise the "home-school option." They pointed him to a web site where he could get a diploma, complete with transcripts. It took McSwane a few days and $200, but he became a proud graduate of Faith High Baptist School.

McSwane did not wear a recording device when he visited the recruiting station, but he did record some of the phone calls from the recruiters. He also got his sister to take a picture of him with the recruiters, and a high school friend with a video camera was across the street from the head shop when he show up to buy the detox kit.

McSwane's article for his high school paper, *The Westwind*, (for which McSwane is editor) ran on March 17, 2005.

But rather than just leave it at that, McSwane called several news organizations. CBS4 News in Denver called him back. The TV station's report prompted the Army to pay attention to recruiting practices across the country. On May 20, 2005, the Army closed all of its recruiting stations so that recruiters could undergo a day of ethics training. It also began an investigation of specific complaints about recruiting practices.

The "something cool" that David McSwane wanted to do turned out to have important national implications.

Jim Stovall (May 27, 2005)

ESSAY: Aristotle figured out the storytelling 2,300 years ago

An article in the March issue of **The Writer** magazine lays out what Aristotle thought about storytelling about 2,300 years ago. The article, written by **William Kowalski,** points out that the Greeks didn't have the novel, but they did have theater. From that, Aristotle decided to outline what he thought made a compelling story:

- All stories are made up of five elements: setting, character, plot, dialogue and thought (intentions/motivations).
- Plot is everything.
- Characters come second.
- Keep the audience interested by making reversals.
- Use discoveries to move the plot.
- The perfect plot is simple, not complex.

Kowalski adds some excellent commentary to each of these points, including this one:

By the way, was it smooth sailing once our ancient student of writing achieved the goal of all literary hopefuls -- publication, or in the case of dramatists, production? Not quite. "Because there have been poets before him strong in the several species of tragedy, the critics now expect the (writer) to surpass each of his predecessors," Aristotle intones.

In other words, 25 centuries ago, authors were already awaiting their reviews with butterflies in their stomachs. Some things never change.

(The Writer magazine article is not available online.)

Dec. 6, 2008

ESSAY: E.B. White and the 'steely modesty' of his writing

Roger Angell is familiar to many of us as the writer of some great books about baseball. He writes with insight and grace, and for those of us who love the game, he had always increased our pleasure. His day job is that he is a writer for the New Yorker magazine. He is also the stepson of E.B. White, and in this week's New Yorker – the magazine's 80 th anniversary edition – Angell has written a gentle remembrance of the man he knew as "Andy."

E. B. White
Graphite drawing by Jim Stovall © 2005

E. B. White is known to literate parents as the author of *Charlotte's Web* and other children's stories. His words and stories have charmed children – and adults – for three generations. They will continue to do so for many more.

White is known to those of us who have studied and taught writing, and tried to improve our own, as the co-author along with William Strunk of *The Elements of Style*, surely the best book of advice on writing, pound for pound, that the 20th century produced.

Angell writes:

Clarity is the message of "The Elements of Style," the handbook he based on an early model written by Will Strunk, a professor of his at Cornell, which has helped more than ten million writers—the senior honors candidate, the rewriting lover, the overburdened historian—through the whichy thicket. "Write in a way that comes naturally," it pleads. "Do not explain too much." Write like White, in short, and his readers, finding him again and perhaps absorbing in the process something of that steely modesty, may sense as well the uses of patience in waiting to discover what kind of writer will turn up on their page, and finding contentment with that writer's life.

The phrase "steely modesty" grabbed my brain as I read Angell's article. I have been preaching modesty to my students for years. "Put yourself in the background," I tell them. "Let the content come forward." But to do that takes confidence and, yes, a certain amount of "steel."

Angell's article, which should be read in full, demonstrates that White lived as he wrote – modestly, patiently and honestly.

Good writers come in various shapes and personalities, and not all are like the patient and modest E. B. White. That's ok. Still, a little patience and a measure of modesty would not hurt any of us.

* * *

The citation is:

Angell, Roger. "Andy." The New Yorker. February 14-21, 2005, pp. 132-150.

(Originally posted Feb. 18, 2005)

ESSAY: "Yesterday, comma, December 7th, comma, 1941 dash . . . ."

On the day that Pearl Harbor was attacked, President Franklin Roosevelt dictated a speech that would become one of the most famous in American history. Unlike more modern presidents, who employ an army of speechwriters, Roosevelt wrote much of his own speeches.

He began this one by dictating the words in the headline above to Grace Tully, his secretary. The first draft of his first sentence was, "Yesterday, December 7th, 1941 -- a day which will live in world history . . . ."

Roosevelt was a notorious and perfecting editor, particularly of his own copy. No one knows what went through his mind when he was writing and editing this speech, but the evidence that he was giving each word much thought can be found in the image above. He made many changes to that draft. To Roosevelt, those first words were important, and they had to be right. They must have sound flat, like the beginning of a dull history lesson.

Somewhere in the process, "day" became "date," signifying a larger and more memorable moment in history than just a day. And "world history" became "infamy." Roosevelt needed a word that would express the outrage that Americans felt about being "suddenly and deliberately attacked."

Infamy was the word he chose. It hadn't come to him at first. It came only in the editing process.

And it has become an indelible part of American history.

References

Brooks, B. S., Pinson J., Wilson, J.G. (2003) *Working with Words*, 5th ed. New York: Bedford/St. Martins.

Bryson, B., (1990) *The Mother Tongue: English and HowIt Got that Way.* New York: William Morrow and Co.

Cappon, R. J. (2003) *The Associated Press Guide to Punctuation*. Cambridge, MA: Perseus Publishing.

Hodges, J.C., Whitten, M. (1999) *Harbrace College Handbook, 13th ed.*, Ft. Worth, Texas: Harcourt Brace College Publishers.

Kessler, L., McDonald, D. (2004) *When Words Collide, 6th ed*. Belmont, CA: Wadsworth.

LaRocque, P. (2003) *The Book on Writing: the Ultimate Guide to Writing Well.* Oak Park, IL: Marion Street Press.

Stepp, C. S. (2000) *Writing As Craft and Magic.* Boston: McGraw-Hill.

Strunk, W., White, E. B. (1999) *The Elements of Style.* 4th ed. New York: Macmillan.

Watkins, F., Dillingham, W., and Martin, E. (1996) *Practical English Handbook.* Boston: Houghton Mifflin.

Zinsser, W. (2001) *On Writing Well. 25th Anniversary Edition.* New York: Harper Resource.

Web sites

American Society of Journalists and Authors, http://www.asja.org/

Power of Words, http://www.projo.com/words/

Poynter Online's "Fifty Writing Tools",
http://poynter.org/content/content_view.asp?id=61811

Writers Write: The Write Resource, http://www.writerswrite.com/

Guide to Grammar and Writing, http://webster.commnet.edu/grammar/

Language Corner (Columbia Journalism Review),

Made in the USA
Middletown, DE
02 September 2018